Straight from
THE HEART II

More True Stories of
Remarkable Encounters with
Once-in-a-Lifetime Horses

Selected by the editors of EQUUS magazine
Foreword by Laurie Prinz

Illustrations by Pamela Wildermuth

PRIMEDIA Equine Network
V.P., Group Publishing Director: Susan Harding
Editorial Director: Cathy Laws
Director of Product Marketing: Julie Beaulieu
Cover illustration: Susan von Borstel
Book Designer: Lauryl Suire Eddlemon,
based on original design by Celia Strain

PRIMEDIA Equine Network
656 Quince Orchard Road, Suite 600
Gaithersburg MD 20878
301.977.3900

Library of Congress Cataloging-in-Publication Data

Straight from the heart II : more true stories of remarkable encounters
with once-in-a-lifetime horses / selected by the editors of Equus
magazine ; foreword by Laurie Prinz ; illustrations by Pamela Wildermuth.
     p. cm.
   ISBN 1-929164-18-1 (pbk.)
   1. Horses--Anecdotes. 2. Human-animal relationships--Anecdotes. I.
Prinz, Laurie, 1962- II. Equus.
   SF301 .S86 2003
   636.1--dc21
                                          2003005495

To order call 800.952.5813
Order online at TheEquineCollection.com

TABLE OF CONTENTS

CHAPTER 3
COMFORT AND JOY

CHAPTER 4
THANKS FOR THE MEMORIES

FOREWORD

For 25 years, EQUUS has been dedicated to helping readers provide their horses with the best care possible. Each month, the magazine reports on the latest veterinary research, presents the advice of leading experts, and explores the physiology and psychology of the horse. But we've always known that there's more to our mission than a simple exchange of information: It's just as important to celebrate the special role horses have in our lives.

There's no better example than True Tales, one of our most popular features. True Tales are heartwarming and often enlightening stories written by EQUUS readers. These stories take many forms—some are exciting accounts of horseback adventures, others are heartfelt tributes to extraordinary horses—but they all remind us of the rare and invaluable bond we share with our horses.

In the *Straight From the Heart* series, we present a sampling of our most memorable True Tales. We would like to thank those who have allowed us to reprint their stories and everyone who has shared a True Tale with EQUUS over the years.

Laurie Prinz
Editor, EQUUS

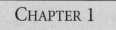

Chapter 1

The Stuff of Dreams

THE PERFECT HORSE

*From years of wishing and dreaming,
she knew just what she wanted—
but would she ever find it?*

BY CHRISTA IACONO

"Easy, boy," I cautioned my mount, as we descended the steep, pine-needle-carpeted hillside. My hands gripped Black's mane as he slipped and slid on the tricky footing. I concentrated on relaxing, breathing deeply and keeping my balance. Luckily, the bottom of the hill was not far away.

At the end of the steep incline, I patted my horse's sweaty neck and vowed to find a better route for our return. Then I tapped my legs on Black's sides, and we trotted over to a nearby lake. My little horse lowered his head to sniff the water. Within seconds, I could hear him greedily slurping. His sides were still heaving from exertion, but otherwise he seemed fine. I leaned back to stretch my aching muscles and enjoy the beautiful morning, a big grin on my face. How lucky I felt.

He was a terrific horse, my Black. He wasn't afraid of anything. He could climb the steepest hills, gallop to my heart's content and neigh on command. Always obedient and happy to be with me, he was my companion and friend on endless outings. I could proudly say I had made this horse all that he was—with my imagination, my black crayons and a scrap piece of plywood. Black was the best make-believe horse a little girl ever straddled.

In time, of course, I outgrew my wooden steed. My first "real" horse experience was with Lady, the stubborn, old white mare who captured my heart at summer camp. No matter how hard you kicked Lady's sides or kissed to her, you would be lucky to get her to walk. I loved her all the same, and vowed to save my birthday, Christmas and allowance money to buy my own horse someday. Maybe it would even be Lady herself.

After three horse-camp summers, I moved out of the city and into the country. There, to my delight, we had horse-owning neighbors. I was 12—a good age to own a horse, I thought. My dad had a different opinion. He said a horse would cost too much money, and he wasn't sure how long my love of horses would last.

I was disappointed, but I didn't give up. The next summer, my mom arranged for me to lease Blaze, an 18-year-old palomino gelding, from the neighbor across the road. Blaze had a great disposition but lots of quirks. It took 30 minutes to catch him in the pasture. His trot felt like riding in a jeep at full speed across a field full of gopher holes. He rarely loped when I asked, and when he did, it was often on the wrong lead. But I was content just to brush him and walk around the arena. The best part was that I got to ride almost every day. This went on for more than a year, until the neighbor sold Blaze to buy a new show horse.

Even more than I missed the old palomino, I missed having my "own" horse. Blaze's former owner said if I bought a horse I could board it at her farm. Not wanting this great opportunity to pass, I pestered my father relentlessly. This time, he told me he wouldn't even consider buying a horse until I had researched the cost of purchasing and caring for one. That lifted my spirits—finally, there was hope my dream of horse ownership would come true!

I prepared a list of questions about the costs of horse ownership, and over the fall and winter, I interviewed my neighbors, asking them things like "How much money do you spend on hay for one horse per year?" I talked to about 10 people, always when my dad was away, so I could collect the information secretly to surprise him.

Early in March, my big day came, and I presented what I had learned. To my delight, my father seemed quite pleased. But then came the famous "what if?" He wanted to know what we would do for boarding if our obliging neighbor moved. He needed a backup plan, he said. OK, I could do that. I made up flyers asking about alternative boarding places and gave them to all the neighbors I had visited previously.

About a week later, I had my backup plan. I had met all the conditions. All I had to do was wait for my father's decision. (I must admit I did a few extra chores during this time and was even nice to my annoying brother, at least when my father was around.) To say I was nervous would be an understatement.

April came, and with it my 15th birthday. All day, my mind was racing, thinking about horses. After the cake and ice cream were gone and I had opened the gifts from my brother and sister, my father reached inside his jacket and handed me a cream-colored envelope. My hands shook so much I could barely tear it open. I pulled out the card inside and read, "Enjoy your new horse!" I just couldn't believe it. I was afraid that any minute now my parents would hand me my usual birthday package, a new plastic model for my horse collection. As realization set in, tears came to my eyes. I was getting my own horse.

We began looking almost immediately. I knew just what I wanted—a Quarter Horse for Western pleasure riding. I called owners and trainers and decorated local tack shops with "Horse Wanted" posters, hoping to find the perfect horse. Little did I know how long the search would take.

There was nothing special or exciting about the first couple of horses I saw. The next few were no better. Before long, I had looked at 10 horses, and none of them seemed right. Then came horse number 11. He was just what I had in mind, and we made an offer. I waited anxiously to hear, but when the call came, it was bad news. The owners had decided to sell him to a relative. We went on looking.

Horse number 18 was Burnie, a roan gelding who appeared to have a nice temperament. We bought him with a 30-day, money-back guarantee. Then the veterinary check turned up what seemed to be a neurological lameness. By the end of the first week, Burnie had run off with me and started rearing in his stall. The decision to return him was easy.

By the time we got to horse number 20, people were telling me I was too picky. We had used up so much gas driving all over southeastern Minnesota that my dad said I could only look at horses no more than 30 minutes away. We began revisiting farms we had already checked out. No luck.

Before I knew it, summer was over. I had seen 30 prospects, and I still didn't have a horse. The equine market began to dwindle. I couldn't help wondering if I should have settled for one of the rejects. Finally, one December evening, long after I had given up hope of finding a horse before spring, a trainer called. She had seen my poster in a tack shop and thought she had the perfect horse for me. The price was twice as much as we were willing to spend, but because the owners wanted their mare to go to a good home, there was hope we could negotiate a better deal.

The next weekend I met Classy, a 6-year-old dun Quarter Horse whose personality matched her glowing golden coat. Her gaits were so smooth that I felt we were flying. She seemed able to do whatever I asked, responding with enthusiasm and a little extra spunk. To make sure she was the right horse for me, I leased her for three months and took some lessons on her. What I loved most, besides her charming character, was her willingness to learn. On April 4, almost a year after my father agreed to buy me a horse, Classy was mine. Since then, she has been my dream come true, my joy in life and my dear and special friend.

My homemade hobby horse, long since retired, still sits in the corner of my room. When I look at him, I think about how far I had to come to get where I am now. I think about Classy, and about how much of my make-believe horse's personality shines through her. Remembering my days with Black, I can see why it took so long to find my perfect horse. Ideal companions don't come along every day. One thing I know for sure: Classy was worth the wait.

THE MAYBE TIME

Ghostly white, the stallion danced in her dreams—
a promise of things to come.

BY DORIS DAVIDSON

I unfold the letter. I read it again. I haven't told my husband. If I accept, I will have to tell him. But first, there is this time when all things are possible.

The letter is from Missouri, from Three Creek Farm. Tré Awain Donoghoo is in Missouri. He is 12, he is white, he is all muscle and bone. His breed has carried Irish kings, hauled peat, starved with the starving. He is a Connemara pony.

I have kept two stallions. I know what that's like. I know, too, that this seventh decade I'm in, when just sinking through crusted snow can be a shock, is not the best for carrying water over an icy path to a steam-blowing, dancing horse.

My face contorts with images of winter, the lugging of hay and water. The outside tap, covered with old coats, is turned off. The five-gallon pail won't fit under the kitchen tap. I fill it in the bathtub. I carry the water down the hall, across the living room, through the patio doors, over the veranda, the sloped and icy lawn. In my mind, I put the pail down to soothe the sloshing water. And to rest. I pick it up. I reach the fence.

"Drink," I command this horse in my head. He grabs the pail

7

with his teeth, half emptying it. He is not thirsty. In an hour the rest of the water will be frozen, and I will worry until I fill the pail again.

And spring! The breeding season. Spring means waking up every morning with dread. Spring means leading the mares down to the stallion's field to see if they are receptive. Donoghoo and the mare must sniff noses. I must not hurry them. I am scared. I want to get this over.

The mare squeals, and the white-stallion-who-is-in-Missouri rears and strikes the fence with a foreleg. Crack! He shakes his head. He races away and comes back fast. His chest pushes against the fence. The wood bulges.

I sweat with him and turn the mare so her tail faces him. The veterinarian says I must not hurry them. He must chat her up.

I push the mare over, line her up against the fence. Donoghoo makes a chuckling sound, warm like toast. He nibbles his way up her back. Her ears flat back, she lashes out with both hind legs. She is not interested. Not today—which means I have to go through all this tomorrow. The mare snatches at the spring grass. I jerk at her halter. She follows me back to the pasture. My shoulder hurts. Arthritis.

But spring will pass. Even this spring that hasn't arrived, that I am living in my mind, will pass. The mares will get bred. I will ask my young friend Heather to help me. She is not afraid. She can make Donoghoo behave, make him do a bit of wooing before he mounts the mare.

And summer will come, when the night wind is a cool hand on my face. I watch this horse that isn't here, his white shape a ghost in the dark. Donoghoo does not trot. He floats. He is the foam on the crest of the wave. His mane rises and settles softly on his arched neck. His tail follows him like a ghost child. I am sick with the beauty of it all.

I must tell my husband about the offer. He does not like big surprises. I will tell him that Laura Balding will lease this horse for two years. I will point out that he is a new bloodline for our mares.

I must answer the letter. I choose the heavy, cream notepaper. Laura already knows I will give her horse a good home, but I tell her again. I say he will stand in a pasture overlooking the lake. Silver himself, he will watch the moon rise silver above the dark hills. (I cross that line out, for fear they might think me odd. Unreliable.) I add that my son dug up a willow tree and planted it in his field. It has grown large and makes good shade. I say Donoghoo will have a bred mare with him for company.

In my head, I hear his call—hollow-soft, alluring like distant thunder. I see his large black eye, the fringe of lashes angled down. He watches me. I tell myself he *wants* to come. I put my pen down.

I look at the field, but not through the glass doors. I go right outside and lean against the gate. It is all so still. So still. Perhaps that is what this decade should be. Time stopped. There is a silence inside me. A waiting.

At my desk again, I ponder the complimentary closing. "Yours sincerely" is always safe. I fold the letter. I put it in the envelope. I do not address it. Nor do I seal it. I put it on the mantel. It sits there. A presence. Charged.

BLACK MIST

*Inspired by a classic children's story and
a little pinto mare, this young rider got to
live out her own happy ending.*

By Kirsten Kauffman

I didn't just read Marguerite Henry's *Misty of Chincoteague*. I *lived* it, both as the third-grader who daydreamed about riding her own pony, and as the teenager who found her longtime dreams coming true.

I had the bad luck to be born an instinctive horse lover in a family of nonriders. Not only would I never *own* a pony, I realized in elementary school—in real life, I didn't even know how to ride. I had little hope that Mom and Dad and I would someday drive to Chincoteague and return merrily to Pennsylvania with a new, wild pony foal, fresh from the island's pony penning and auction, stowed in our pickup camper. Instead, I restricted myself to fantasy, living out Henry's tale, imagining myself taming the famous Misty and exploring the island beaches on her spotted back. As the years galloped past, my beloved Breyer Misty model grew more battered with each imaginary pony roundup, and my copy of the book became more seamed and worn.

Finally, at nearly 14, I won permission to take riding lessons. Bouncing around the arena on the placid school Appaloosas, I slowly gained my seat and discovered the wonders of the real horse world. Within a year, fantasy had become reality, in the form of a leased Quarter Horse-cross mare—until a falling out with the owner left me once more with only books and Breyers. That was when my 4-H leader stepped in, breathing life into dreams I had never taken seriously myself.

The leader's name was Kendy Allen, and she invited me to come and ride at her farm, where she bred and raised her own line of Chincoteague ponies. Chincoteague ponies? That was almost as good as a trip to the pony auction, I thought. Kendy knew Western pleasure was my interest, she said, and she had a green-broke mare who would be perfect for me.

"Her name is Black Mist," Kendy told me as she walked me down the lane that led to her hillside pasture. "She's just turned four, and she's about 13.2 hands tall. That's her—the black pinto."

Black Mist certainly was eye-catching: Her splashy black-and-white coat stood out against more humdrum shades of chestnut, palomino and gray as she played "boss mare," driving her herd-mates around the field. I watched, captivated. "I think we can find a Western saddle your size in the barn," Kendy offered. "You know, there's a 4-H fun show in a few weeks." And so I leased a pony and became an apprentice trainer.

Black Mist and I both had a lot to learn. We spent many hours together in the pasture on the hillside, working on neck-reining and loping and collection. The would-be horse owner in me blossomed, and I rapidly began to cherish affectionate feelings toward "my" mare. Over the next couple of years, we would go from trying our luck in local gymkhanas and fun shows to pinning in district competition. Once we traveled to the state 4-H horse show, where my friends Kerra and Erika showed their pair of young ponies to halter championships, and Black Mist and I competed against the best Western pleasure ponies in Pennsylvania.

It wasn't our day to pin, but we were proud to be there.

Between shows, we three riders (known to our families as "The Three Musketeers") spent long, hard hours at Kendy's farm, stacking hay and digging post holes. And when our work was done, whatever the season, we snatched all the trail time we could get—galloping bareback across neighbors' harvested cornfields or plowing through snowdrifts that reached up to tug at our boots.

Kerra and Erika switched mounts on occasion, trying out this pony or that, but I jealously reserved Black Mist for myself. I loved the way she would jog around the ring with nary a bounce, or charge courageously up rocky slopes and leap fallen logs on the trail. She taught me patience when my right-lead take-offs would not shape up or when our pony-ride fund-raisers ran a hot hour too long. She made a rider out of me, carrying me over my first jump (three feet to clear a downed tree, a leap that nearly left me in the mud), sharpening my reflexes (like the time a pasture full of cows prompted a saddleless Black Mist to spin and bolt), and helping me learn the timing and coordination it took to command a winning performance from her.

All through my high school years, Black Mist was my closest companion, teaching a young woman who had despaired of ever having her own mount what horse ownership was all about. I was dreading the fall of 1996 when, with college looming, I knew I would have to pass Black Mist along to a younger 4-H rider. But before that day came, I would get to live out the last and greatest of my childhood fantasies.

The town of Chincoteague was planning a big summer festival to celebrate local attractions, and the architects of the event had invited Kendy's ponies and riders to make a guest appearance. On the appointed day, a hot morning in June, we loaded Black Mist and her companions into the red stock trailer and drove to Virginia. I couldn't believe I was really going to see Misty's home and the island beaches I had ridden so many times in my mind.

Our festival performances passed in a blur. I recall only heat and bright sunlight and the scent of pine trees, and a luncheon of complimentary platters of steaming shrimp. We Musketeers were waiting for just one thing. The following morning, with official permission, we trailered our mounts to Assateague Island National Seashore, home to the herds of wild ponies who were their distant relations.

As Black Mist and I crested the dunes on Assateague and saw the ocean, the mare pricked her ears and snorted, drawing in the scent of salt and hearing the crash of the waves. I pressed my bare heels against her sides, and together we ventured into the world of a grade-schooler's dreams. I shook my head in disbelief as I plunged my mount into the foamy Atlantic and raced Kerra and Erika and their mares along the golden stretch of sand.

So what if Black Mist hadn't come home with me from the pony auction? I thought. There had been no need to round her up—she had been bred and born at a farm just minutes from my own home. Maybe she wasn't mine, but I had trained her and loved her and would never forget her, and this was ownership enough for me. And here I was, riding her on the beaches of Assateague Island.

On that blazing summer morning, it mattered not at all that the legendary Misty, the pony I'd longed to tame and ride, had died years before. My mount was Black Mist, the fiery little mare who had entered my life so far away and seemingly by chance. As I galloped her across her ancestral island home, I was still living a piece of my childhood dream. For Black Mist wasn't just another Chincoteague pony—she was the great-granddaughter of the most famous of them all, Misty of Chincoteague.

FIRST LOVE

To an 8-year-old girl growing up in a Midwestern town, the big, black carthorse was a creature of romance and legend.

BY SANDRA BLACK

It's Tuesday. He's coming! I hear his *clib clop, drag, clib clop, drag* cadence on the brick-paved street. I spot him now and shout for Magu, "Come on!" She'd better hurry if she wants to get the best bananas.

Magu's my grandma. She's roly-poly round and speaks with a potato-thick Warsaw accent, and she's the best bargain picker in town. But I don't care about the bananas or the bargains. I'm just there for *him*, my first love.

Every Tuesday, steady as rain, the old man and his horse pass through the neighborhoods of Springfield, Illinois—down Miller and Reynolds streets, around to Carpenter, where Magu and I live, and on toward 11th Street. That's how the old man makes his living, peddling fruit and vegetables left over when the main groceries clean their produce shelves.

Slowly the creaky black wagon shudders to a halt. Magu waddles out, determined to be the first to inspect the goods. I'm already there, snuggled up close to the horse.

He is a big, black creature, with a cloud-white star set perfectly in the middle of his wide forehead. That's my name for him, Star. I stroke his whiskery nose, and he whuffles into my hand, seeking the sugar I sometimes sneak to him. I run my hands over his broad shoulders, as high as I can reach, and down his tree-trunk-sized legs. He's so beautiful, so grand. I bury my nose in his neck. He smells very good, of leather and salty sweat. I wish, as I do every Tuesday, that he were mine.

Magu and Darrell's grandma poke through the bananas, looking for the not-too-ripe ones, and shuffle through the oranges to find the fruit with no rotten spots. They chatter and cluck to each other, asking the old man "How much?" and protesting when they think his figure is too high. He mumbles into his mustache, backing down on the price.

The fruit-and-vegetable man is of Bulgarian extract. They say he's lucky he "got out of there" when he did. With his shoulders hunched over and his tiny eyes almost hidden by bushes of gray eyebrows, he's sort of spooky looking. But I think that's just his outside shell, because on hot days like this he quietly chips away at the block of ice in the belly of the wagon, giving cool slivers to us kids hanging around, and only snorts and acts like Billy Goat Gruff when too many of us try to jump on the running boards of the wagon.

I let the buzzy drone of chatter go by as I suck on the ice and twiddle with the horse's ears, feeling his slick, wet skin under the headstall. He stands patiently and obediently, grateful for this bit of respite in spite of my fussing. He works very hard. I wrap my arms as wide as I can around his chest. His huge head hangs over my shoulder, and his breath puffs warm and wet down my neck. I close my eyes, and for a few seconds I am lost in a vision that will remain a vivid memory when he is gone. For this moment, Star is mine and mine alone.

Behind my eyelids, the harness buckles and snaps give way

and the heavy leathers slip from the horse's body. He shakes loose from his bridle and bit. Fire comes into his eyes; smoke steams from his nose. He prances sideways, and I vault like a Plains warrior onto his back. He lunges forward. I bury my hands in his mane, clutch his sides with my knees. We have become one soul. Thunder rumbles as his hooves strike the bricks, and suddenly he is airborne, a black Pegasus against the sun, with dusky raven wings strong as a hundred eagles. He takes me where I've never been before, far from the forest of wooden houses where I live.

Slowly I open my eyes. We are still on Carpenter Street. The horse still wears his harness. "If you were mine, Star, I would brush all the dust from you," I whisper to him. "I would bring you golden apples and never let anyone hurt you." I promise him everything. The fairy tales spin from my mouth like silk webs.

Magu has her bounty in her arms. She prods me to "let go the horse now." She chuckles to the old man's back. "Sanda, she love the horse. Maybe from her grampa, my Frank, she gets it. He was cavalry man. Nobody else in family love horses like Sanda." I release the horse. The old man is already climbing aboard and lifting the reins, clucking him forward. I watch the horse until I can no longer see him, not even his shadow—until the drumbeat of his rubber-shod hooves gives way to silence.

Inside my chest there is a bittersweet hurting, and I promise myself that someday I will have a horse of my own, a great and noble horse, just like Star. Someday. In the meantime, I'll be right here again next Tuesday, waiting. As steady as rain.

Editor's note: Sandra Black didn't have to wait long to realize her wish. When she was 13 years old, she got her first horse, a Quarter Horse mare named Queen Jo Jochebed. She has since owned many wonderful horses.

AN UNDYING PASSION

*Tragedy separates the author from horses
for 15 years, but she eventually found she has
to be with the animals she loves.*

BY TERRI HAYS

My sister Robin was a fearless free spirit. Five years older than I,
she was also my best friend and surrogate mother, and she shared
my passion for horses. Her death devastated me. Although it happened 25 years ago, not a day goes by that I don't think of her.

All three of the girls in my family were horse-crazy, and every
weekend Robin and I would take the bus to visit a friend of a friend
who had horses. We would ride for hours. I was 9 at the time, and
Robin was 14. Robin was amazing; she'd taught herself to ride at
about age 7, and there was nothing she couldn't do and nothing
that frightened her. She rode with what seemed to me to be the
utmost in confidence, while I, the more timid child, rode with cau-
tion if no less enthusiasm.

My sisters and I dreamed of the day when we might each have
a horse of our own, but only Robin was able to fulfill that dream
during our childhood. After years of saving, she bought
Shenandoah, a beautiful, dark-bay gelding with four white socks
and a gorgeous blaze of white. He was an ex-barrel racer who
seemed very calm and reliable.

Robin and I were still on the bus every weekend, but this time we were heading for the stable where she kept Shenandoah. The owners of the barn were a very nice young couple who loaned me an old pony so that my sister and I could ride together. A new highway was being built nearby, and each day we would cross that road to the trails beyond. These were the woods of Staten Island, New York, and back then it was more like a forest to me. Among the trails and back roads, we would ride and laugh together for hours. Despite our age difference, we were best friends.

But as the months passed, we gradually drifted apart. One reason is that I had lost a great deal of confidence when Shenandoah frightened me. One night, he had trotted to the end of the arena with me, then he suddenly spun 180 degrees and took off at a canter back to the gate. My short legs could not even reach the stirrups at the time, and I was completely out of control. Robin made light of it and told me I did fine. She pointed out that nothing bad really happened. However, nothing could induce me to ever ride that horse again.

The other reason my excursions with Robin dwindled in number was that she was beginning to yearn to be around her own peers—other teenage riders who shared her interests.

I remember that terrible day vividly. I was sitting on the front stoop of my house when the owner of the barn drove up. He raced past me and into my house without even knocking. I remember thinking that this was most strange, because he wasn't exactly a friend of the family. Then I heard my mother scream.

Back in the 1970s, no one I knew wore safety helmets on horseback. It just wasn't done. Riding on the paved streets was accepted, and if it wasn't exactly safe, no one really thought much of it. My parents were never concerned about Robin's riding without a helmet. They just did not know any better. No one did.

That day, like so many that had gone before, my sister had

headed out for the trail with a group of riders. They were crossing a paved street on the way to the unbuilt highway when Shenandoah suddenly reared and spun on his hind legs. Robin fell and struck her head on the curb.

The next week was simply hell for my family. My parents went back and forth to the hospital morning, noon and night. Finally, Robin was pronounced brain dead, and my parents were advised to take her off of life support and let her go. It was the most devastating day any of us had ever experienced.

For many years after Robin died, an intense guilt consumed me. I had a huge problem: I still loved horses, and I still yearned for a horse of my own. But my parents were adamant that I should never ride again. Although I would still sneak away to the livery stable every chance I got, I felt terrible that I so loved doing the very thing that had killed my beloved sister. Eventually, I discovered boys and abandoned my dream of ever owning a horse.

Then, when I was 24, my passion resurfaced. After I moved to San Diego, it seemed that I began encountering horses at every turn, and then I realized why I was feeling so empty: I *needed* horses. I bought my first horse in 1990, learned to ride properly and have not stopped since.

Today, I own two wonderful Paint Horses who are my pride and joy. And I am not guilty, because I know that Robin would not have wanted me to give up on something that is as important to me as breathing. I'm positive that she would want me to be happy and to keep my passion alive. Sometimes I try to explain to non-horsepeople that my horses are not a hobby but a way of life. They don't always understand, but I know Robin would have.

SWEET REUNION

Separated from her dream horse, a woman learns the virtues of working with equine imperfection and is doubly rewarded in the end.

BY BECKY HABAK WITH AMY K. HABAK

Lori, my trainer and barn manager, walked out of her office with a big smile on her face. "That was just Keri's mother on the phone," she said. "Sweetums is for sale."

"Oh, I'll take her, I'll take her!" In the barn aisle, I threw my arms around Sweetums' neck and vowed to buy her, even before hearing the price. I had waited a long time for a chance to own this horse, and as joyful as that moment was, I had no idea how many disappointments waited ahead before that dream would come true.

Sweetums was an 11-year-old Appaloosa mare boarded at the stable where I taught riding lessons. The small, stocky mare was out of place among the lanky Thoroughbreds and appendix Quarter Horses that filled most of the stalls. But she had quickly become my favorite.

I got to know Sweetums after an earlier owner replaced her with one of the more stylish Thoroughbreds common at the barn. That's when Keri got her. She was excited about her new horse and did all the things a 12-year-old girl is supposed to do.

She bought pretty, new halters and fancy blankets, and she showered Sweetums with treats. Sometimes Keri just sat in her horse's stall talking to her. What a lucky girl, I thought enviously. I wondered if she realized what she had.

I had wanted a horse of my own since my first ride as a teenager. I rode other people's horses sporadically back then, and I didn't learn much about riding correctly. After I married, I talked to my husband about buying a horse, but we couldn't afford it, so I shoved my dream aside to focus on raising our two children.

When my 10-year-old daughter expressed an interest in horses, I was elated. Together we started taking lessons at the stables, and we both really enjoyed it. Still, we were always riding other people's horses. My husband's only comment was, "You can have a horse when the kids are out of college."

Meanwhile, Keri was growing less interested in Sweetums as boys and school activities lured her away from the barn. When I noticed how much time the horse was spending in her stall, I offered to exercise her for Keri. It was a win-win arrangement: Her horse would get exercised, and I would have a horse to ride whenever I wanted.

I quickly fell in love, Sweetums was so much fun to ride. Her sides and mouth were supersensitive, and she helped me refine my skills. She was versatile enough to ride both English and Western, and we even did some jumping. Except for the occasional spook, she did pretty well on trails, too. But best of all was her canter: smooth, even, floating; it was just like riding on a cloud. I felt secure on her and could hold the correct position easily. She made me feel good *and* look good.

I told Keri several times to let me be the first to know if she ever decided to sell Sweetums. But even though Keri spent less and less time with her horse, she didn't put the mare up for sale. I satisfied myself with just riding her, rationalizing that I had the best scenario—a horse to ride and no board to pay.

Finally, the call came. Keri's mom wanted to let Lori know they'd decided to sell Sweetums, and Lori told her she already had a buyer.

I was so excited! Finally, at age 43, I would get my very own horse; on top of that, it was a horse I already adored. Quickly, I tabulated the expenses, examined my savings and talked to my husband. The sale was set. Then everything came to a screeching halt.

That night, Keri's grandparents called to tell me they didn't want Keri to give up her horse. They agreed to pay the board so Keri could keep Sweetums. She wasn't for sale after all. But the worst news was that they'd be moving her to another barn, closer to Keri's home. That way, they hoped, Keri would be able to ride her mare more often.

Disappointment like no other washed over me. I thought I'd finally realized my dream of owning the one horse I wanted more than any other. Now, in one short phone call, not only was my dream crushed, but I wouldn't even get to see Sweetums any more.

My life went on. I took lessons with my daughter, rode trails with friends and worked with other people's horses. None compared to Sweetums. Through the grapevine, I heard that Keri still wasn't finding much time to ride. Several times over the years, when I ran into Keri, I let her know I was still interested in her mare, but somewhere along the line, I gave up.

Four years later, I bought a horse. Sally was a 10-year-old Appaloosa mare I found living out her life in a field at a Paint breeder's farm, where she served as an occasional trail horse for kids. When I learned that she had been trained by Mel, the same person who trained Sweetums, I decided to give Sally a try. Mel assured me that she would be a good horse.

But Sally was far from what I'd hoped my first horse would be. I continually compared her to Sweetums, and Sally was far from measuring up. Although she was smooth, she lacked the flexibility and responsiveness that Sweetums had. Because Sally had spent eight years doing little more than hanging around in a field, she needed refresher training, and Mel and I spent many months working with her. It was also a training period for me. I had to refine old skills and learn new ones. I had to constantly think ahead to maintain control of her shoulders. Sometimes I couldn't even turn her. And the canter—forget it. Sally was strung out and unbalanced. She rarely picked up the left lead. I felt like every ride was a fight. Nothing seemed right, and I regretted buying her. After a particularly trying day, I ended up in tears.

"Stick with her," Mel said. "She'll make you a better rider." Sure enough, Sally and I gradually learned to work things out. She improved in the ring, and as long as I didn't ask her for the left lead, she remained fairly calm. (We later learned that a cataract was forming in her left eye. Since she couldn't see as well going that direction, she was afraid to canter on that lead.) She learned how to travel correctly on the bit, with rounded back in a dressage frame. Her trot became very light and airy, and her stubbornness dissipated. I had to admit, she felt good. Her canter would never be "riding on a cloud," but at least her trot was somewhere close.

But it was on the trail that Sally really won me over. She gave me courage when I lacked confidence. She stayed calm when I was nervous. When she was energetic, I was still able to control her. Her little spooks were few and far between, and I felt much safer riding Sally on the trail than I ever had on Sweetums. Sally grew on me, and as difficult as she could be in the ring, I loved her for our trail rides.

Just as I was learning to love Sally, I heard that Sweetums

was for sale. Keri was now 19 and engaged to be married, and the couple decided to sell the horse. My heart jumped, then paused. I already had a horse.

"So, get another one," my daughter said. She now had two horses of her own as well. "Why not?"

The wheels were turning in my head. I could swing it financially if I moved Sally down to the farm where my daughter's horses were. But why have two horses in two different places? It seemed frivolous.

"You can ride Sally with me at the farm, and Sweetums at the barn. Sweetums is better in the ring anyway, and that's mostly what you do there," my daughter rationalized. She knew how important favorite horses could be.

I couldn't bear the thought of selling Sally, not after all we'd gone through together. She had become my favorite trail horse. But I couldn't let Sweetums pass by, either.

I was finally able to decide after my husband weighed in, suggesting that I make Keri an offer. "Okay!" I screamed. Given my last attempt to buy Sweetums, I didn't breathe a sigh of relief until the bill of sale was signed and in my hand. Finally, my favorite horse was mine.

I've now had Sweetums for a year and Sally for four. Sweetums is everything I remembered, and I now appreciate her talents even more. But I enjoy both my horses, learning from each one and appreciating their unique personalities every day. Both have shown me the rewards of perseverance—dreams do come true. Better late than never.

LOST AND FOUND

Eight years away from horses is not enough to extinguish a passion that is in the blood.

BY ANNETTE ISRAEL

"Just wait until she turns 16. When a boyfriend or a car comes along, little girls say 'So long!' to the horses."

"Not my kid," my father said quietly and confidently to his brother, my uncle Karl. And he was right: It didn't happen when I was a teenager. But it *did* happen. When I was 36 years old, I walked away from horses for what I thought would be forever.

They say we are born to it, this love of horses. And I now know that it truly is etched into who we are. I cannot remember *not* loving horses as a child. My mother used to tell me that when I was just a year old I would occasionally stand transfixed in front of the television. My parents soon realized that I did this only when horses were galloping across the screen. I would fall asleep on my rocking horse. My childhood was filled with drawing horses, reading every horse book in the local library and rejoicing when I received horse books as gifts. I collected statues. I wrote down pages of names I thought of for horses. I saved every horse hair I happened to find. I collected horseshoes. I lived in anticipation for the weekends, when I would get to go to the local riding stable for a one-hour ride. I would come home glorying in the magnificent smell of horse. I could mimic a horse's every sound and movement. I dreamed about horses night and day.

One day when I was about 10 years old, my mother found a bucket in my closet: "What's this for?" she asked.

"It's for when I get a horse," I said. The bucket was filled with odds and ends of stuff that I figured one could use for a horse: some nice, soft cleaning rags, a toothbrush, a dog leash, my mother's (missing) vegetable brush, an oval hand-size dog brush and a real horse brush that Papa had found for me. My mother gently tucked the bucket back into my closet.

When I was 12, I said a very special prayer and asked God to let me have a horse before my 13th birthday. I never mentioned my prayer to my parents at the time. But they were keeping a secret from me, too: Day by day, they were edging closer to the realization that my passion was far more than a passing childhood fancy. "She's lived with this constant heartache for 12 years," my mother told me, years later, she had said to my father. On December 5, 1968, a spirited part-Arabian bay mare named Velvet came into our lives. The next day I turned 13.

Velvet was feisty and full of herself 24 hours a day. She taught me to ride and to respect the power of a horse. She was also my first, "best friend" horse. Like many youngsters, I joined 4-H and tried my hand at different disciplines of horsemanship.

When I was 15, I convinced my parents to let me have a second horse. Out riding one day, I had seen a weanling Arabian colt in a pasture, and I'd stopped to ask about him. Yes, he was for sale. I told the man that I'd be back the next year to get him. "Sure, kid," he said. My parents agreed to the second horse, but there was a hitch: I would have to buy the colt and pay for all of his *and* Velvet's upkeep. It took me a year to save up the money. I sold my bike; I walked the neighbor's dogs and cared for her cats.

I raked leaves. I shoveled snow. I saved up $200 and was able to buy the colt for $175.

Mc-Keever turned out to be a distinguished show horse. I trained him myself, and he never took less than first place in halter at Class A Arabian shows. He qualified for the U.S. Nationals four years in a row in halter. I took him to Louisville once, in 1980, to show him in the National Championship gelding halter class. We didn't place, but standing in that ring with the nation's finest Arabian geldings, I had one recurring thought: *"I wish I could tell everyone here that I paid $175 for him."* "Mac" also excelled in hunter under-saddle classes and in dressage, in which he earned a U.S. National Top Ten award in 1983. I lost him to colic in 1984.

As a young adult I earned extra money by training horses and giving riding lessons. Eventually, I acquired a breeding stallion and several mares and operated my own small farm. I could not count all the horses I owned over the years, and my stallion sired many fine foals. I am thankful that I was also able to rescue many horses who were destined for slaughter; I spent some time with each one before sending them on to loving families of their own. All of my life, horses were synonymous with my name, and even though I also had a career as a police officer, *everything* I did revolved around horses.

But in 1991, 20 years after Uncle Karl's predicted cut-off date, my horse world came to an end. It wasn't because of a boyfriend. It wasn't because of a car. It was just—because. I simply walked away. I gave away each of my beloved horses, entrusting them to people I believed would give them lifelong care.

Over the next eight years I did many new things with my life. I focused more on my writing, earned a Master's degree, returned to the violin and made new friends. Horses never even crossed my mind—except on certain blustery winter mornings around 5:30, when I would think of "all those crazy horse people" out in their barns, chipping ice out of water buckets. Me, I would snuggle up tighter with my little dogs and go back to sleep. Eight years is a long time.

In the spring of 1999, though, I started waking in the middle of the night thinking of the one horse I had loved most, a gelding named Zester. Before long, he was on my mind constantly, day and night, and I knew I had to see him again. I made a call and learned that my old horse, now 17 years old, was not where I thought—he'd been gone for two years, and no one knew where he was. I launched an all-out search that summer for Zester, a chestnut with four white socks and a big blaze. I hired a detective, posted a reward, and drove all over the state following his trail. As I tracked him from owner to owner, I learned some nauseating facts: He'd been shipped through several auctions and had developed some nasty habits along the way. People told me they'd been unable to saddle or bridle him at all, or, once he was tacked up, they wouldn't be able to untack him. I also learned that his auction prices were getting perilously close to slaughter rates.

As the months passed, the goal of my search gradually changed. I had to do more than just see him—I wanted him permanently back in my life. I started buying horse things again: buckets, feed tubs, a navy-blue halter and an assortment of brushes. I would have given anything to have him back.

Then one day, I found him. Zester was with someone who had purchased him at yet another auction, undoubtedly saving his life. I went for a visit, but he was distant when I stroked him, and I'm not sure whether he remembered me. I made a generous offer to buy him on the spot, but it was refused. I'm not sure why, but apparently the new owner didn't want to sell him just then. I later learned that he was resold to someone else. I was happy to have had the chance to see him again, and to assure myself that he was OK, but ultimately I was unable to get him back, and I had to let him go.

Now here I was with a houseful of horse things and the beginnings of a new notion: *Why not get a horse?* I remember one day when the UPS man came to make a delivery. "What's all this farm stuff?" he asked as he glanced around my small home. There was a 50-gallon water tank in the kitchen, a wheelbarrow parked against the sofa, and tools like pitchforks and rakes standing in a corner.

"It's for when I get a horse," I replied.

That October I found Maali, an Arabian mare—a chestnut with four white socks and a big blaze—and she's the sweetest being I've ever known in my life. I didn't ride her before I bought her because, you see, I wasn't planning on ever riding again. Oh, no. I just wanted a horse to lead around, smell and touch. But then one quiet evening, when the two of us were all alone, I climbed up on her, bareback. It had been almost 10 years. Instantly I was flooded with tears, and many moments went by while "my little angel girl" just stood there quietly, flicking her ears back and looking at me in that quiet way horses do.

It wasn't too long before I bought a saddle. I chose a Western model, because I wasn't going to get back into dressage, and I certainly wasn't going to show—not ever again. Oh, no. But soon Maali began to show me that she has quite a stride. She also emphatically informed me that she hated the Western headset. So it was back to English tack, and before long we began easing back into dressage. When Maali, too, seemed to be missing the company of horses, I found Bonnie, an equally gorgeous (and sweet) true-black Arabian mare. The next spring, I took the mares to a show to compete in halter classes, and we did very well.

So here's the rest: I sold my car to buy a truck and a horse trailer, and "the girls" and I headed back to the show circuit. At age 45, I am as excited to spend time with my horses as any kid in 4-H. A wonderful family stables my horses nearby, and I am out there two or three times a day doing all my own chores including, yes, chopping ice out of buckets in the wee hours of cold mornings. My next major purchase will be my own property. It is as if I had never been away. It seems like it was someone else—someone I read about in a story—who lived those eight years away from horses.

So, yes, we are born to it. This love—this flame, this whatever-you-want-to-call-it—can never die. Those of us who share this passion want to be around horses, but it is much more than that: We *belong* to this magnificent creature who shares our lives so willingly. It is the natural flow of our lives.

WHEN IT'S IN THE BLOOD

*"The girl who loves horses" always will—
no matter what the years may bring.*

By Jan Hare, PhD

When I was young, I read all the *Black Stallion* books, faithfully tuned in to "My Friend Flicka" and rode a broom with the bristles threaded and tied with fresh roses. Occasionally, my friend and I would coax our parents into attending "rodeo" performances. We'd never been to a real rodeo or any other equestrian event, but we loved to put on these performances. We would enter the "ring" riding our brooms in an enormously extended trot, then we would canter tirelessly round and round and round. Finally, we'd take a victory gallop around the far perimeter of the yard and close with a deep bow to the wild applause of our imaginary audience and—I imagine—the heaving sighs of parental relief from boredom.

Remembering those summer evenings, I'm quite sure I was always more horse than rider. Riding a broom is a complex experience in dual identity; your legs belong to the horse, your head tosses a flowing mane, but your hands hold the reins, and your voice continually speaks to your mount: "Whoa, buddy. Easy now."

Since those summers 40 years ago, my life assumed a pattern like that of many other women: children, career and a life-altering divorce. Mine is not a unique story, but it is the story of many girls who are now approaching mid-life.

I once was a little girl who loved horses—*loved* horses. This emotion is distinctly different from the fondness many children have for horses. True lovers of horses read horse books, dream about horses, draw horses, pretend to be horses and walk for miles to feed carrots to pastured horses. True lovers of horses grow up into people who, to the astonishment of spouses and friends, weep at the sheer beauty of the Budweiser Clydesdales as they gallop across the television screen. ("It's only a beer commercial," says the husband. "Why are you crying?") These may be embarrassing moments, and few understand them except for those women who once were little girls who loved horses.

Only one of my three children inherited this oddness. My other two certainly like horses well enough, but only the one has the passion, the fire that runs through her veins and never leaves. I first recognized it when she was a toddler on her rocking horse—her eyes glazed over, she was clearly elsewhere. When she outgrew the rocking horse, she tacked up a broom and set up a jumping course. I remember thinking, "Uh oh. There it is."

Eventually a Thoroughbred came into our lives and changed us forever. Many people know this story, too. A stroll around the grounds of any horse show reveals many women like me: We help groom while the children get dressed, we polish boots, we cheer from the fence, we cool down the horses, we celebrate with our excited winners, and we hug away their tears when they finish last. In between comes the steady pleasure of mucking stalls, cleaning buckets, grooming, feeding and loving a particular horse. And then we work overtime to pay for the next show. My daughter cultivated her riding abilities—skills that I like to think I too might have been able to develop, except that my life just did not happen that way.

A snapshot of our lives today now shows this mother and daughter in different places. Now, it is I who smells of horse sweat and she who, fresh out of college, is immersed in an academic job and trying to decide whether to continue her studies. She is torn because this passion that unites us now torments her. A promising career in medicine lies before her, but still she longs to devote her life to riding, mucking stalls and taking care of a horse. Doing both isn't an easy option when you're 21 years old, you're not wealthy and you live in a big city on the East Coast.

She is in that oh-so-familiar place of young adulthood—trying to decide how to be faithful to her passions while learning to support herself. Which is the path of greatest integrity? Which path will cause fewer regrets over lost opportunities? This is a conflict of privilege, I realize, but it is painful nonetheless.

More than anything else, I want her to learn to believe what I believe, and my message to her and anyone like her is this: Once this passion is in your blood, it will never go away. Your life can wander away for a while, but remarkably, the horses will be back someday. My daughter fears that all will be lost if she doesn't have horse sweat on her hands every day, starting right now. She is young, and she doesn't yet understand how strong her passion is.

Each day my morning begins with a 6 a.m. stroll to the four-stall barn in my backyard, and the time I spend caring for my horses is as deeply satisfying as I always imagined it would be. My daughter's Thoroughbred gelding is living out his retirement here, along with another retired Thoroughbred jumper. There's also a Norwegian Fjord horse, who carries me on trails and pulls a sleigh in the winter, and a Pony of the Americas, who also loves the trails as well as local parades.

My equitation is decent if basic. And although I didn't become the rider I wanted to be, my daughter did. And if she ever has children, it will not surprise me to hear her say, "I did not be-

33

come as accomplished a rider as I wanted to be. But my child did that."

There are many of us out here—mid-life women who once were girls who loved horses. Some of us stayed with horses throughout life and became accomplished riders, trainers and breeders; some like me simply ride trails and hold "beauty parlor Saturdays" in the barn. We are all still in love.

Four gleaming horses graze outside my front window. I know every inch of their bodies, and they are fastidiously groomed although they rarely leave home. They cavort endlessly in the pasture, and I swear they really do seem to be aware of me as I sit on the deck in the evenings with a glass of wine, an appreciative audience of one, because they put on a magnificent performance. Someday, in response to my enthusiastic applause, I expect to see four lovely bows.

CHAPTER 2

TRIED AND TESTED

THE GREAT ESCAPE

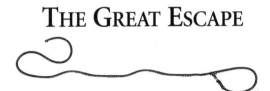

*A high-speed leap from a trailer onto an
interstate highway wasn't enough to defeat
a horse as tough as Tonka.*

BY NANCY ORTH

Tonka Tuff walked quietly up the ramp into our two-horse trailer. Finally, after a 10-month search, my new horse was coming home. Tonka, a 4-year-old Missouri Fox Trotter, was just the horse I needed to continue competing in endurance trials; after I'd recovered from a back injury, my doctor and I agreed I would need a gaited horse.

I secured the panic strap to Tonka's halter, put the butt bar in place and locked the ramp, which formed a four-foot-high rear door. Soon my husband, Paul, and I were out on I-72, driving from Pleasant Plains, Illinois, toward Cincinnati, Ohio. Tonka settled down almost immediately, munching from his hay bag and occasionally looking over his shoulder out the rear of the trailer. The upper doors of the trailer had been removed, leaving a "window" across the back, about 24 inches high, between the top of the ramp and the roof.

About an hour into the trip, we passed through a noisy construction area, where the roadway became bumpy and uneven and the trailer "bucked" a bit. Looking back through the mirror, Paul commented that Tonka was turning his head to look back. I didn't think much about it because I knew I had fastened the panic release strap securely to his halter. Soon the road smoothed out and we were back to our highway speed of 50 mph. Suddenly, we both felt a hard, jarring movement; when I looked out the rear window into the trailer, my heart stopped: My horse was gone!

A black pickup truck pulled up behind us with its horn blaring. We pulled over, and the man driving it told us he'd seen our horse jump out of the trailer, and he offered to take me back. Grabbing a lead, I jumped into the truck; the driver did a U-turn across the median to head back to where he'd last seen Tonka. As we searched, the driver told me that at first he thought the horse was a deer on the roadway; he'd managed to avoid hitting him, and when he'd realized what had happened, he'd sped up to catch us.

We found scrapes on the pavement where Tonka's metal shoes had hit the road, but the horse was nowhere in sight. We found a manure smear where Tonka had apparently left the pavement, but I could not find any hoofprints in any direction, either in the gravel or the grass. The roadside grass was chest high, so we could not see into the ditches very well. Behind me, traffic was racing by at 60 mph in both directions. It seemed like the horse had disappeared into thin air! Even worse was the thought that, if he wasn't dead or dying hidden in the ditch somewhere, he could be miles away by now, and he could run panicked back into traffic.

Then I saw him. Or thought I did. In the distance beyond four lanes of highway, there was a bay horse with his head down, grazing. I crossed the highway only to see a foal by that horse's side. My heart sank.

By the time I managed to run back across the highway, an Illinois state patrolman had stopped to help, and he'd called for assistance. With several of us working now, we continued to search through the grass and bushes up and down the shoulder. Finally, a policeman walked up to me and said, "Ma'am, we've found your horse!"

I ran to where he pointed, and I couldn't believe my eyes! There stood another police officer, the pickup driver—and Tonka! Tonka was standing! Despite his pain, he'd allowed the pickup driver to approach him and attach a belt to his halter as a lead rope. I attached my own lead and gave the man back his belt. I tried, but I couldn't thank him enough for all his help. He simply said, "I can't stand to see an animal hurt," and then he headed to his truck and went on his way. In all the confusion, I never did get his name.

Tonka had survived falling out of the horse trailer at 50 mph. But he was unwilling to put any weight on his right rear leg. He was standing in direct sun, and the temperature was hovering in the lower 90s. Assessing his injuries, I saw he had multiple patches of hide gone from all his lower legs, a terrible hematoma developing, and a possible broken right hip. He was in terrible pain.

Paul arrived at the scene about this time. (With the trailer, he'd had to go on down the highway before he could find a place to turn back.) He got out the cell phone and called Stacy Bowman, the woman who'd just sold us Tonka. She called her veterinarian, who referred her to Wade White, DVM, an equine veterinarian closer by. Bowman then left work, went home, hitched her trailer, loaded a "buddy" horse and set out to help us.

Meanwhile, I sponged Tonka to help cool him down and covered him with a fly sheet. With a stethoscope, I could monitor Tonka's vital signs. His heart rate was an amazingly low 56 beats per minute—but his respiration was at 120 breaths per minute. I talked to him, trying to calm him down, but he was going into shock, and he started colicking. He pawed the ground vigorously. Checking for gut sounds, I heard only distant, infrequent sounds in one quadrant out of four. He was not interested in eating or drinking, nor was he interested in his surroundings. I knew that if he went down, he would never get up. With much coaxing, I was able to move him about 10 feet to a shade tree, out of the direct sun. Gingerly, he put some weight on his right rear leg.

Finally White arrived. Wasting no time on formalities, he listened for gut sounds, checked the mucous membranes and ran back to his truck. He returned quickly with three huge syringes and injected Tonka with pain medication and sedatives. Tonka dropped his head a bit and slightly closed his eyes as the pain eased. Then the veterinarian inserted a tube through Tonka's nose into the stomach and pumped three gallons of electrolytes and mineral oil into him to reverse the colic.

Not until the immediate crisis was over did White stop to talk to me. He told me that Tonka was obviously in terrible pain, but he didn't think anything was broken. One of those injections had included penicillin to ward off any infections, and White sprayed the multiple abrasions with fluorescent yellow Furacin spray. Soon Tonka started stomping at flies and moving around a little, acting more like a horse again. I mentioned that I had bought Tonka to be my endurance horse, and White replied, "If he could survive what he just endured, nothing on the endurance trail should bother him."

Judging by the hoof marks on the highway, it looked like Tonka came out of the trailer headfirst. Then, he apparently "skated," twisting and turning more or less upright for about 300 feet before he hit the pavement on his right hip. Thankfully, this little stretch of pavement was smooth blacktop unbroken by any joints or other rough spots.

Inside the trailer, it looked like Tonka had somehow

released the panic snap attached to his halter. With his head free, he apparently managed to get a front foot into the manger, maybe both feet. He then turned himself around, and with center divider and butt straps still intact, climbed over the securely closed, four-foot-high ramp door and out the back of the trailer.

Soon Stacy Bowman arrived with her trailer and "buddy" horse. With much coaxing, Tonka slowly walked the 50 feet across a deep drainage ditch to the roadside, where he—amazingly!—stepped right into the trailer. Grateful that our horse had survived his ordeal, Paul and I followed Bowman back to her farm.

White and Bowman's regular veterinarian, John O'Keefe, DVM, had agreed that Tonka would fare better in a small paddock rather than a stall to minimize stiffness as much as possible. By that evening, he was dragging the right rear toe due to the pressure from continued bleeding into the hip. He was reluctant to move at all, even when we attempted to hand walk and let him graze on lush grass. A few hours later, he was dragging the entire rear leg. He wouldn't move from one spot; he'd just pivot in place in the paddock.

When O'Keefe examined Tonka the next morning, he felt that the hematoma was still developing and that to cut it open now would cause only more internal bleeding as well as opportunity for infection. He suggested waiting a few days before draining it and said that it might have to be drained several times; not draining it could cause permanent scarring of muscle tissue. But the veterinarian seemed pleased that Tonka was moving around as freely as he was less than 24 hours after such a trauma; the horse might be able to recover fully. As O'Keefe filled out his bill, I couldn't help but smile at how he'd spelled Tonka's name: "Tonka Tough!" How appropriate.

Our story ends well. Stacy Bowman and her husband insisted that we leave Tonka in their care until he was ready to travel.

O'Keefe came out twice to drain the hematoma, and the swelling subsided dramatically. The gelding's superficial wounds also healed nicely, although Tonka will always bear some scars to remind us of his ordeal.

Finally, the day came when Bowman e-mailed to tell me how Tonka was actually galloping around the paddock as though nothing had ever happened, and soon O'Keefe announced that Tonka could travel—just 24 days after the accident.

The lesson I learned was to always be prepared. Now, when I travel with horses, I always make sure I have a cell phone, emergency medical supplies and a list of phone numbers that includes my home veterinarian as well as veterinarians and hospitals local to my destination. It's also important to have a bill of sale that specifies who owns the horse as soon as he steps into the trailer and to have full insurance coverage that begins the moment the horse is yours. And, when trailering a new horse, I attach the panic snap to the trailer, not to the halter, and I make sure I have full back doors that are securely in place; carrying along a buddy horse who's a seasoned traveler is also a good idea. Most of all, I've learned to expect the unexpected any time I load a new horse into a trailer.

SKY'S SURPRISING RESERVE

A hot mare becomes a cool customer when
an accident traps her in an overturned trailer.

BY THERESA IRETON

When I first met her, Sky was a mare full of fire with a lot of issues to work through. I was looking for a younger horse but something about the almost-black appendix Quarter Horse caught my heart (even if my brain was left out of the loop), and I spontaneously decided to buy her.

In four years, I've never regretted that decision. Sure, there were many times that I doubted my abilities to train and handle her properly, and she is still a hot horse. She now walks quietly out to her barrel patterns, but it takes only a twitch of the rein for her fire to burst to the surface. Her extreme sensitivity and responsiveness to even the lightest of cues sometimes gives a person the unsettling feeling of riding a stick of lit dynamite, yet she has become the eager and fun yet quiet and controllable barrel horse I wanted her to be.

It is hard to believe that a horse with this much fire could have a level head, but she has proved it to me several times now. She once stood for hours tangled in barbed wire before she was rescued, and she escaped without a scratch. When she cast herself, she lay quietly until we could pull her far enough away from the wall to allow her to rise. Neither of those incidents, however, compares with what happened to us in January 2000, when Sky showed me what a treasure she truly is.

I was returning to college at Washington State University in Pullman after Christmas break, a seven-hour haul almost completely across the state. Sky had come home with me for the long vacation, and now I was taking her back in my two-horse straight-load bumper-pull trailer.

Heading out, I knew I'd face one serious challenge in the road ahead. We had to cross White Pass, a high mountain pass that had recently received several inches of snow. But we reached the pass and got through with no troubles, and the rest of the trip would be all blue sky and dry pavement—an easy drive. Or so I thought.

Dusk was falling as we arrived in Colfax, only 28 miles from Pullman. Our trip was almost over. As we picked up speed on the other side of town, I thought I felt the trailer shifting a little as we rounded a few corners. The road seemed dry, but it was hard to be sure, and the dropping temperatures could make even a slightly damp road slippery. I picked up my CB to ask my boyfriend, Scott, how the driving was. He was out ahead of me somewhere in his pickup; he told me he was doing 45 mph with no problems and hadn't noticed any slipperiness. That reassured me. If Scott's light pickup wasn't having traction problems, then certainly my heavier Blazer, carrying the weight of the trailer tongue on its rear tires, would be just fine. I wish now that I had listened to my own instincts.

While doing 35 mph, I caught up with a truck that was going quite a bit slower. I hesitated, wondering if he was going so slow because he thought it was slippery, too, but then I remembered that Scott was going much faster, so I decided to pass the truck. The passing lane was clear, so I touched the gas, and the powerful engine responded. As I shifted to the left, the rear end of the Blazer suddenly kicked out to the right. Unworried, I steered to correct. Nothing happened. I steered more sharply. Suddenly I realized something had gone horribly wrong. I still remember the sick, powerless feeling that filled me as we started to slide sideways. The horse trailer swung around until it was beside me, then it pulled the rear of the truck around as it passed me, jackknifing, and we spiraled sideways and backward across two lanes, into oncoming traffic. I didn't have time to be scared. Then, abruptly, we were out of pavement, and for one eerie moment, we were airborne.

With a crash of breaking glass, the Blazer landed heavily on its passenger side and slid a few feet in the mud. Stunned, I closed my eyes for a moment, thinking, "This isn't happening. It has to be a dream." Numbly, I turned off the engine and looked out into the ditch illuminated by headlights. Then reality came rushing back. Frantically I found the CB and screamed for Scott. Panicking, I struggled to get out, not realizing that I was still wearing my seatbelt. With the headlight buzzer sounding in my ears, I ripped off my seatbelt and immediately fell onto the passenger door. Scrambling to get up, I heard Scott's voice answering on the CB, and I screamed that I needed him here NOW! I flung down the mike and managed to push open the Blazer's heavy door. A blast of cold air struck me as I frantically climbed out.

A woman was standing on the side of the ditch, shouting something at me. "Is there anyone else in the vehicle? Are you alone? Are you okay? I sent my husband to call 911."

I looked at her blankly as I leaped to the ground. She spoke to me again. I paused. What was wrong with her? Couldn't she see how desperately I needed to see my horse? "MY HORSE! Oh my god, my horse!" I suddenly realized I was screaming. The trailer was deathly silent. Ignoring the woman, I fought back panic as I sprinted and stumbled, half sobbing, to the trailer lying on its side in the ditch. Suddenly I remembered the sounds I had heard during our sickening spin across slick road; Shy had been scrambling in a panic in the out-of-control trailer, and I desperately tried to avoid thoughts of why the trailer was now so completely quiet. Uninvited pictures crowded into my mind—Sky lying in a pool of blood, Sky twisted in a crumpled heap with a broken neck. "No! Don't think it!"

Rounding the corner to face the back of the trailer, I stopped short. Sky's door, on the driver's side, was pushed out almost six inches and the latch was mangled. I couldn't open it. Still no sounds came from within. Whimpering, I looked at the other door, trying to press all the horrible images out of my mind. I ripped open the passenger-side door and let it fall to the mud like a ramp. I stopped short when I heard the sound from within.

A nicker. It was Sky's usual "I'm ready to get out of the trailer now" nicker. I almost sobbed with relief, knowing that Sky was still alive, but still I feared I would find her down, unable to rise, in a tangled mess, possibly with broken bones.

As carefully as I could, I ducked under the stuck door to crawl into the trailer. As soon as I was inside, I paused again, almost dumbfounded with amazement. Sky was standing. The inside of the trailer was a chaos, with rubber floor mats and hay strewn everywhere. Sky must have fallen at least once. Her withers were crammed against the side—now the ceiling—of the trailer, and her head was turned far to the right and lowered to avoid the center divider. There was absolutely no other way she could have gotten to her feet in the contorted space, but she had done it. And now she was standing quietly, waiting to be let out.

Almost sobbing with relief, I tried to examine her in the near darkness. I could hardly see, but about then an older gentleman walked up with a flashlight. I probably wouldn't recognize him if I saw him again, but I remember his easy, comforting presence, his work-callused hands, and his gentle manner with my horse. Sky was relatively unhurt. Fortunately, I had not tied her, but her halter had caught on something and took the skin off of her face in several places. Several scrapes on her legs were bleeding, and she had one cut under her jaw that later needed to be stapled. We were very lucky.

My next impulse was to get her out of that trailer, but it took only a second to realize that I couldn't. The center divider at the rear of the trailer was now a chest-high barrier. Sky wasn't going anywhere.

Scott arrived. Suddenly I remembered that my two cats were still in the Blazer. Scott climbed in and found one of them trapped under my laundry basket; the other, terrified, was running back and forth. Both were unhurt. Scott put them in his truck, and together we waited for help to arrive. Sky took all of this in stride. She became upset if she was left alone, so I stood with her, stroking her and trying to regain some measure of composure. As long as I was with her she stood quietly, occasionally shifting her weight to relieve the pressure on her withers.

The state police arrived and immediately called the fire department. Once they arrived, they examined the trailer and decided the center support beam had to be cut away. We decided to use a torch, but since they would be working so close to Sky's hindquarters, they would need to sedate her first. Finding a veterinarian was a challenge, since it was after 8 p.m. on a Sunday. Finally we located one, but she was more than 20 miles away.

And so we waited. The firemen found a nice couple about a quarter mile away who said they would take Sky for the night once we got her out. With the panic finally ebbing, I tried not to think about the damage to my truck, which I had spent the entire summer working on, nor about the mangled trailer that we had just finished restoring and painting. But I was immensely glad that I had spent the extra money to replace the glass windows with Plexiglass, which stood up under Sky's weight.

It was almost an hour before the veterinarian arrived and gave Sky an injection of Rompun. The gentleman who had been with us from the start offered his bandanna to cover Sky's eyes as the firemen cut my trailer apart with their torch. She never flinched as the noise, sparks, flashing and smoke assailed her from only a few feet away. Once I thought her blanket would catch fire as the sparks flew within inches of her haunches, but Sky never moved.

Finally, they lifted away the door and pulled out the divider. The state patrol officer had been concerned that Sky would bolt out of the trailer the moment she could, so I was ready, holding her with a long rope. Sky, however, backed down the door/ramp as though she were unloading any old place. Her withers caught on the lip of the door and she nearly stumbled, but she recovered and calmly stepped backward out into the cold darkness. In her drugged state, she leaned heavily on me as we staggered toward the distant barn, but I could not have been more proud of her. I couldn't imagine any other horse, especially one as high-strung as Sky, walking away from that accident with only superficial wounds.

The next day, the barn owner where I board Sky came with his trailer to carry her the last few miles of her journey. I was worried about loading her, and I wouldn't have blamed her if she'd never wanted to go anywhere near a trailer again. But she stepped right in as though nothing had happened. Once again, I was so proud of her I nearly burst, and I was ashamed that I had doubted her confidence.

Over the next few months, my dad and my brother put my

trailer back into working order. It certainly isn't pretty, but it is functional, and we triple-checked it to make sure it was roadworthy. The first time she saw it again Sky loaded right in. Fear still grips me when I think about that accident, but Sky seems to have perfect confidence that I will not allow her to be hurt, and she trusts that getting into the trailer is a good idea. She amazes me. Truly, she is one in a million.

People still tell me that my horse is too high-strung, that she can be crazy and too full of energy. I can't deny this—Sky can be one hot little mare. But I have also seen her face down tremendous danger with a cool and collected manner that would shame the most bombproof of horses. She may have given me reasons to doubt her as I struggled with her training over the years, but I am glad that I never gave up on her. She has rewarded my perseverance more thoroughly that I could ever have hoped.

ORDEAL BY WATER

*When a trail rider and her mount topple
into a flooding river, luck, instinct and a few
good friends save the day.*

BY MARGARET KRASTEL

I couldn't wait to go on the Red Deer River ride. A longtime
member of TRAC, the Trail Riding Alberta Conference, I was
thrilled to be back in full swing with my 11-year-old Arabian
gelding, Allimar. The previous year, colic surgery had kept Alli
out of competition. But this year he seemed "fit as a fiddle." Just
two weeks before, he had earned a respectable fifth place—
despite a shaggy coat that caused him to sweat more than
usual—at the season's first ride. Now it was early June, and a
slick and shiny Alli was ready for more challenges. Because the
ride had been new to our circuit last year, I had never been to this
part of central Alberta, and I was looking forward to the change
of scenery and trails.

The morning was beautiful as only an Alberta spring
morning can be. My friend and riding companion, Sue Harris,
and I rolled and tied our jackets behind our saddles at the first
pulse and respiration check. Sue was riding her 7-year-old
Connemara/Arabian gelding, Irish, Alli's stablemate and best
friend. The two traveled well together on the trail, although Alli

consistently had to pace himself one gait faster to keep up with his buddy's huge stride. At 15.3 hands, Irish dominated 14.2-hand Alli in every way except age and pecking order.

At home, Irish was Alli's "herd." My little horse supervised his companion's comings and goings in the pasture, making sure he didn't get too close to the rest of their field mates. Once, when Irish had snagged himself on a sharp stick in the woods, Alli led me to him—walking ahead of me, just out of reach, and then standing and waiting for me to catch up. Irish recovered from that injury and was now doing well on our Competitive Trail Ride circuit. He and Alli remained a devoted pair, and although their bonding was a nuisance at times, on this day it would help to save Alli's life.

About half an hour after the veterinary check, we turned a corner on a grassy path to find the mighty Red Deer River in full flood just ahead of us. It was an awesome sight! The water was brown and angry-looking, with fallen trees, fence posts and other tumbling debris racing by. This was undoubtedly the spot ride manager Dave Firminger had warned us about at last night's briefing. The riverbank would be unstable here, he'd said. We were not to take the trail close to the water's edge, but a second trail, higher up, near the trees and brush. What no one had foreseen was that unseasonably warm weather earlier in the week would cause the mountain snowpack to melt quickly, raising the river four to five feet overnight. The lower trail was nonexistent, and the upper trail was in danger of being obliterated by the rising water.

Walking slowly ahead of Sue and Irish, Alli and I came to the point where the trail curved up into the brush, away from the torrent. As we were about to swing into the trees, Alli paused and eyed the water lapping at the trail's edge. He lowered his head to take a drink. What happened next will remain frozen in my mind forever. Before his lips could touch the water, the ground beneath us—weakened by the undercutting current and the dozen or more horses who had already traveled over it—began to move. Slowly, as if in slow motion, the earth sank into the river, carrying us into the icy torrent.

Alli rolled onto his side. As I came off, the current grabbed me and tore me away from the bank. I was propelled downstream like a piece of driftwood. Gasping for air and struggling to keep my head above water, I remember thinking, "No one could survive this." Then another voice inside me said, "Swim, Margaret! Swim!" I looked toward the bank and saw that I was being carried farther out into the river with every second. Quelling my rising panic, I began to swim steadily toward the bank—not fighting the current, but going with it. With each stroke, I was closer to gaining my objective.

I am not a strong swimmer, but the adrenaline push in my body gave me strength to reach the shore. Grabbing at the first overhanging branch I saw, I felt a surge of dismay as it broke off in my hand. The next branch was stronger, however, and despite the current's pull, I managed to haul myself over to the bank and crawl out. I got to my feet in thick brush with only one thought: Alli!

I ran back about 75 yards to the spot where we had fallen in. As I crashed out of the bushes, the look on Sue's face was one of utter surprise. She was sure I had drowned. Sue was on her knees, holding Alli's bridle reins, keeping his head above the muddy water. The rest of his body was submerged. As I ran toward them, Alli struggled to get his front feet up onto the bank's edge, but to no avail. He seemed to be tiring quickly, and I wondered what chance we had of getting him out of there.

Just then, the last two riders in the Open Division, young Braden Brooks and Brent Firminger, came around the corner and gaped with amazement at the sight of us. Brent jumped off his horse and tried to help Sue at Alli's head. At that moment, I noticed what appeared to be a big stick jutting out of the water by my horse's left shoulder. Quickly, I lay down on the bank beside his head, stuck my arm in the water and felt a big piece of root jammed up under his breast collar. When the earth gave way beneath us, it must have exposed a huge tree root, and one of the branches had pinned Alli to the bank's edge.

Somehow I managed to break off a piece of the root with my bare hands and pull it from under the breast collar. Alli was free. He made a valiant attempt to leap up onto the bank. But as he came out of the water, the current caught him, flipped him over backwards and ripped the reins out of Sue's hands. I watched, horrified, as my special little horse was carried swiftly toward the center of the river, with only his head poking out above the waves. Overcome with anguish, I collapsed on my knees and covered my eyes. A stunned silence followed, punctuated only by my cries of grief. Suddenly Sue exclaimed, "Marg, he's up! He's found some footing out there!"

I raised my head and looked in amazement. Across 100 yards of raging river, Alli was on his feet and trotting upstream in our direction through fetlock-high water. Apparently, the current had swept him against the flooded edge of a low-lying island, and he had managed to haul himself out of the river. Now, more puzzled than concerned, he looked across to where we were, trotted upstream to survey the situation there, and then came back. Positioning himself where he could see his buddy Irish, he seemed to relax. I'm sure he was confident we would come and get him any minute. He appeared unhurt, and although I was still worried that he would get a leg caught in the reins or try to swim the river, I began to relax, too. Sue took command. She sent Braden and Brent back down the trail to get help, made sure Irish would stay where Alli could see him, and kept talking to me calmly the whole time. Neither of us had any idea how we would get Alli off his island perch.

Now the novice riders, who had started just after our open division, began to come around the corner. In pairs and groups, they stopped to witness the drama unfolding on the grassy river-bank. Once again, Sue took command, diverting them from the fragile brink and up onto the remaining trail. I briefly wondered what might have happened to them if Alli and I had not fallen in. Grace Cottreau, our dear friend and riding companion, was in one of the groups. With no hesitation, she elected to forgo the ride and lend us her support. While this was going on, Alli made one attempt to get back to us. He waded into the river, but when he felt the strong pull of the current, he retreated to solid ground and stood again, calm and relaxed.

After what seemed an eternity, I heard the sound of a truck. A pick-up drove into the clearing, and I breathed a sigh of relief. Though I wasn't sure how anyone could rescue my little horse, seeing Dave O'Callaghan and Tim Tufford—both experienced horsemen and woodsmen—get out of the truck made me feel immensely better. Dave and Tim decided that the only way to get to Alli was by boat. Once they were on the island, one of them could then ride or lead the horse to a spot where the crossing would be safer. They roared off in the truck, planning to knock on any and every farmhouse door they came to until they found someone who had a boat.

Brent and Braden, who had summoned this help, now returned. As the last group of novices passed by, Brent spied his dad bringing up the rear. Dave Firminger's look of disbelief when he saw the swollen river made me realize just how fast the water had risen. The previous afternoon, when he had come by to check the ribboning for the ride, both trails had been visible and dry. Dave knew the area well and felt he might be able to cross over to Alli's refuge from a point farther upstream. He rode off in that direction, with Brent close behind.

We stood there, Sue, Grace, Braden and I, keeping an eye on Alli and making sure Irish stayed in his line of sight. By this time, we had resigned ourselves to being spectators. Suddenly, something caught Alli's attention. Peering upriver, we saw a canoe coming toward us—a tiny canoe, in that huge, boiling river. It occurred to me that Tim and Dave O'Callaghan were risking their lives to save my horse. Because the sight of them might startle Alli, they beached their craft far upstream on the bar and slowly started wading toward the horse. Alli calmly stood his ground. When Dave took hold of his reins, the breath I had been holding came out of me in a great "whoosh." I felt incredibly relieved, even though they still had to get Alli out of the river.

Dave mounted my little horse and rode him along the flooded sand bar toward a curve in the river he'd decided might make an easier crossing. We watched horse and rider negotiate the water-covered island, dipping in and out of sight, until they finally climbed a short bank about half a mile away and disappeared from view. All of us whooped with joy. We assumed they were safely on the other side of the river. (Little did we know they still had the main channel to cross.) We were still hugging each other with delight and relief when we heard the sound of a horse racing toward us. Around the bend came Brent Firminger, fear and concern on his face. "Come quick, you guys!" he yelled at us. "Dad's horse is under water!"

Sue and Grace mounted and took off after Brent, while I ran as fast as I could behind them, dreading what we would find. As I came out into the clearing, I saw a knot of people standing quietly with Dave Firminger. There was no sign of Tar, Dave's horse. I knew my worst fears had been realized. As Dave described it, the two had tried to cross a deep pool in the river, and Tar had panicked when he felt his feet leave the ground. Instead of swimming, he went under the water, in an attempt to gain his footing, and drowned. Emotion overcame me, and I began to sob. Trying valiantly to save my horse, this man had lost his. It seemed totally unjust.

While I struggled to control my tears, the others were making plans about what to do next. Since we had passed the halfway point of the morning ride, Sue and Grace decided to continue down the trail to base camp, where all the riders would stop for lunch. I would drive back to the camp in the truck with Dave Firminger. There we would pick up a horse trailer and set out to rescue Dave O'Callaghan, Tim Tufford and Alli, who were—we believed—on the other side of the Red Deer River, waiting for a ride home.

Meanwhile, out in the river, another drama had been unfolding. When Dave O'Callaghan and Alli disappeared from our view, Dave was heading to a quieter spot along the river where he felt they could swim across, back to the bank where we were. Alli was not completely happy with this plan, but with Dave's coaxing and expert horsemanship, he finally took the plunge and started swimming. All went well for several minutes, Dave told me later, but when they got to within a few feet of the opposite bank, Alli decided he had had enough. Sliding off the panicking horse into the cold water, Dave was close enough to shore to be able to clamber out. But Alli turned around and swam all the way back to the island.

As he emerged from the river, my horse was now well upstream from where we had originally gone in—and from where he had last seen his buddy, Irish. Perhaps he spied Sue and Grace across the water, winding their way down the trail. Desperate to get back to his "herd," Alli trotted to the end of the sand bar and then—as Dave and Tim watched in disbelief—launched himself into the flood. He careened down the middle of the river, the current pulling him to an unknown destination. Only his head was visible to the two men, and even that disappeared a couple of times before he was out of view. They were sure that would be the last anyone would see of Alli. They felt bad about having to tell me the river had claimed my little horse.

What happened next, none of us will ever know. The secrets of that blank space of time are locked in Alli's memory. All we know is that somehow he got out of that river. Sue and Grace were winding their way back to camp when Irish suddenly spooked and whirled to look behind him. There came Alli, galloping down the trail at full speed, reins flying and tack flapping. His ordeal over, he slid to a stop beside his buddy. He did not appear to be hurt, but he was soaking wet from the tip of his ears to the bottom of his tail. Down at the camp, still looking for a trailer, Dave Firminger and I heard the news from an incoming rider in time to greet the little troop as they arrived.

How Alli managed to survive with so little damage I'll never know. A thorough exam revealed sore muscles in his right loin and a few scrapes on his right shoulder and hip, corresponding to some deep scratches on his breast collar and the stirrup leathers. Perhaps he tangled with something as he came down the river. A dose of bute made him more comfortable, and we left him loose to graze. With Irish tied up, none of us worried that he would wander off and leave his buddy.

Once we got home, I gave Alli a week off and then picked up our conditioning program again. Two weeks after the incident, we competed and placed at the Drayton Valley Ride. The trail there included several high, muddy river crossings, and my heart was in my throat the first couple of times. But Alli just waded in with no hesitation at all. Mind you, he had a good example to follow. He was traveling close behind a big bay gelding named Irish.

Epilogue: Dave Firminger's sacrifice touched many hearts. Trail riders are generous people, and on the evening after the ride, TRAC president Brent Seufert passed the hat. More than $600 was raised, and I'm happy to report that Dave now has a fine new horse.

DISAPPEARING ACT

*On a dark and stormy night, a newborn
foal goes missing from her stall.*

By Jenny Hamilton

Foal watching is something that all horsepeople approach with a mix of emotions. There is the agony of sleep deprivation after a regular day of hard physical labor. There is also the anticipation of watching foals running and playing in pastures with their mothers. To a horseman, this is pretty much how we imagine heaven— although maybe with a good riding horse and a few dogs thrown in for company.

So there is something magical about the birth of a foal. The long, wobbly legs. The big doe eyes. The sense of wonder we get when such a magnificent creature allows a bond with people. It's impossible to ignore the wild nature of horses during foaling time, because mares don't look for human guidance; even the most faithful old friend will usually give birth in the most inconvenient time or place, often in the dark of night. Somehow, that bit of wild instinct just makes us realize how special horses are to let us share anything at all with them. Magic.

Late one summer night, though, I was to witness an entirely different kind of foaling magic: the rabbits-disappearing-into-top-hats type of magic. It was a night I'll never forget.

Some friends were going out of town for a week, and they asked me to house- and horse-sit for them while they were gone. Their mare was two weeks overdue with her first foal. No problem: I had worked around horses my entire life, and I had attended a few births, though always with more experienced people around. But I felt ready to meet the challenge.

After the first several nights, I was pretty well settled into the new routine: Every hour I would wake up to check the mare on a closed-circuit television monitor by the bedside, and then I'd drop instantly back to sleep. One evening, at about bedtime, a good summer thunderstorm rolled into the area, and I thought to myself, "I bet tonight is the night." Before going to sleep, I reviewed the baby basics: I had phone numbers for veterinarians and other numbers for more experienced horse midwives; I knew what the placenta should look like, I knew to call for help if a nose and two front feet did not come out first, and I knew that a healthy foal will stand and nurse within an hour of birth.

Since I had been waking hourly for several days, I didn't have any trouble getting to sleep, and when the alarm went off every hour, I dutifully checked the monitor and turned up the sound to listen to the mare.

At 10 p.m., all was well.

At 11 p.m., still no changes.

At midnight, everything was still fine.

At 1 a.m., everything was all wrong. The mare was frantic, spinning in circles and screaming. Lying in the middle of the stall was something that looked roughly like afterbirth. I could see no foal. Hoping that what I was seeing was a wet spot created by a broken water pipe—and that maybe there was a loose horse outside upsetting the mare—I leaped into my boots, grabbed the flashlight and phone, and ran to the barn.

There were no loose horses or broken pipes. The wet spot in

the middle of the stall was definitely afterbirth. And there was absolutely no sign of a foal. I quickly reviewed everything I knew about biology and concluded that it was impossible to have the afterbirth before the birth. I was still ready to call a veterinarian for help, but the problem was that I had no idea what kind of help to ask for.

I wouldn't say that I panicked, but some pretty strange ideas raced through my sleep-addled head. The foal had been eaten by wolves. The mare was a medical freak. Or, perhaps, UFOs did exist and aliens had abducted the baby. Meanwhile, the mare was still whinnying and spinning in her stall.

Then Spot, the farm's dalmatian, suddenly started barking out in the darkness. Not that I overreacted, but now I was back to the eaten-by-wolves scenario, and I was sure the whole pack was still outside. (The fact that there are no wolves in Maryland was beside the point.) With portable phone in one hand and flashlight in the other, I went out to do battle with the foal-napping terrors of the night. Bravely, I headed toward the barking.

"Spot, where are you? Watcha barking at?" I quavered.

It was dark and still raining. As I swept the area with the flashlight, the beam caught two things. One was Spot, still barking, not too far away. The other thing I saw in the darkness, just beyond the dog, was a pair of huge green eyes, hovering a couple of feet above the ground. I couldn't see the body behind them, but it was definitely dark-colored, and those eyes were definitely bear-size, and they were bear-height above the ground. (We do have bears in Maryland.)

Spot was bravely holding the creature at bay, and having heard plenty of bear-eats-dog stories, I worried for her. I walked up behind her, hoping to be able to grab her collar and pull her back to safety. Suddenly the mysterious eyes started bobbing up and down. Letting loose a string of profanity that would make a

Marine blush, I snatched at the dog. Still facing the thing-in-the-dark, I started to back away, dragging Spot with me. (I might possibly have been mumbling something that sounded a lot like "trucktrucktrucktruck!")

At this point, as if kind Mother Nature was trying to soothe my frazzled nerves, a CRACK of lightning hit a tree less than a mile away and lit up the world. In the flash of light I saw the animal we faced. My "bear" turned into a tangled-up newborn foal, her head bobbing as she struggled to get to her feet. Just as quickly, all was dark again.

The little filly must have rolled under the stall gate and staggered away until she collapsed. Now she was terrified and weak and lying out in the rain. I squatted down and talked to her quietly until I could get close enough to touch her. She was still struggling to get to her feet, now mostly so that she could get away from me. I put one arm around her chest and one under her haunches to pick her up. As she tried to coordinate her legs, I carried her back to the barn where Mom was still calling frantically.

In fact, the mare was the next problem we faced. She was so upset that I could not get the gate open—every time I opened it she pushed it closed again as she tried to reach me to nose her baby. Finally, I timed the gate opening so that I could get fully inside during one of the mare's whirls, while she briefly had her backside toward us. Then Mom bodyslammed us into the wall as she finally connected with her wayward child. Her screams turned instantly into deep contented nickering, and her violent licking of the baby proved that, here at least, absence had made the heart grow fonder.

Unfortunately, the nickering and nosing also turned out to be our next hurdle. A foal needs to nurse within its first few hours to get the necessary colostrum. This mare was too frazzled after the separation to let the baby get more than six inches from her nose.

Every time I nudged the foal back toward the udder, the mare turned to keep the foal in sight.

After several minutes of futile circling in the stall, I decided to change tactics. I got a lead rope and tied the mare to one of the beams in the stall, then I helped the foal stagger back to the mare's hind end. The little filly eagerly started sucking on everything she could touch: my arm, the mare's tail, the mare's leg, my arm again, the mare's stomach. I was wondering if she would ever get it right when finally she latched onto the teat. Then it was as if I was holding Popeye in my arms as he eats a can of spinach. I could feel the surge of strength flowing into this wobbly little creature, and within a minute, she did not need me to help her stand. Mom looked back and nickered. Magic.

TERROR ON THE TRAIL

*A young filly is put to the test when a peaceful outing
becomes a struggle to save a beloved dog's life.*

BY JUDY LOVATT

I always save up some vacation time to use in October, the best
month for horseback riding in western Michigan. It was on one
of these treasured days, at the end of my favorite month, that I
had the worst experience of my life.

The wind was blowing hard. The temperature had dropped
and rain was on the way, but I was determined to ride that afternoon. With only two weeks left until deer-hunting season, every
chance was precious. I saddled K'Pio, my three-year-old home-
bred Morgan filly. Usually, my daughter would ride out with us,
but today our only companion was Hobbin, my large boxer. The
filly was still early in her training, and I planned a short, calm ride.

K'pio did well on the first part of the trail. It began to rain,
but that was a minor inconvenience. We would be home in 30
minutes. We crossed onto National Forest land and headed down
the two-track to the place where it splits into two trails. I chose
the right fork—K'Pio had been on that one before—and started
the filly into a trot. Hobbin loped along just in front of us. Feeling
his age more these days, he was content to stay nearby and skip
investigating on his own.

We were going at a good pace when I spotted a man and a woman coming toward us on the trail. They were just around the corner, at a place where the path circles between two swamps. I am sure that Hobbin, running ahead at ground level, did not see them. I pulled K'Pio to a stop, worried that the strangers would spook her, and called out to the dog. Then I started to turn around and backtrack to the fork we had just passed.

Before I could complete the turn, I heard a shot and a yelp. Looking back, I saw Hobbin running toward me. At first, that seemed normal—he always catches up quickly when we change direction. Then I saw blood pouring from his face. Behind him the man was in full pursuit, swearing and yelling. The woman ran after him.

Terrified, I shouted, "What did you do?"

"No dog is going to attack me!" the man screamed as he ran toward me, still cursing and waving his .22 rifle.

I couldn't believe this was happening. "We ride all over these woods, and he never attacks people!" I yelled back. "He is just an old, friendly dog! Would you have shot me next, when I came around the corner?"

For several minutes we argued, while Hobbin, still bleeding, circled my horse's feet. Finally, the hiker declared that he would shoot the dog and "put him out of his misery." His companion, silent till now, suddenly spoke up. "Hurry home, and take him to a vet!" she urged me.

"How am I supposed to hurry home?" I asked. "I live miles from here." The woman began to cry, but the man ignored her. When he pointed his gun at my dog, I knew it was time to get out of there. Still crying out in fury and despair, I rode back down the trail, and Hobbin followed.

We hadn't got far before he lay down. It was raining steadily by now, and very cold. I got off the filly and sat next to him. He stretched out his body and closed his eyes. I was sure that he was mortally wounded, and I decided to just stroke him until he died. Amazingly, my young, inexperienced horse did not run off. Usually, she was so impatient that it took great effort for her just to stand still. This time, she waited quietly in the cold rain.

After a few minutes, Hobbin got up and moved to a different spot. His breathing got very labored. I sat next to him, tears streaming down my face, waiting for him to die. But he didn't die. Fifteen minutes later, he got up and started walking around again. At this point, I realized that I should try to get him home. Holding K'Pio's reins, I picked Hobbin up—all 90 pounds of him—and began to walk. It wasn't long before I had to put him down. Too heavy. I would never make it out of the woods that way.

I had to think of some way to make this work. I looked around for something I could drag Hobbin on—nothing came to hand. I lined K'Pio up beside me and tried to get the dog up on the saddle. The filly actually stood still for this. I lifted him partway up, then pushed until he lay across the saddle. But as soon as K'Pio stepped off, Hobbin slid down the other side. I caught him just in time and lowered him to the ground. Now what?

If I put the dog's back legs up first, I decided, his head would be on my side of the horse, and I could support him. With a mighty effort, I got Hobbin's rear end over the saddle. I rested his head on my left arm and held K'Pio's mane with my left hand. My head and shoulders were covered in blood. He looked right at me, and I believe he understood what I was doing. Time to get going.

I maneuvered the filly toward a little rise and pulled myself into the saddle. But everything felt wrong. The right stirrup was next to my knee, and the left stirrup had disappeared below my outstretched foot. The saddle had slid sideways as I pulled myself up. Holding Hobbin and trying to keep K'Pio calm, I worked to push the right stirrup down. No luck. The dog was in my way, and I could hardly breathe with the effort this was taking.

Deciding to ignore the stirrups, I asked K'Pio to move. She managed a few steps, then started fussing. I peered around Hobbin and saw that the saddle was nearly totally upside down beneath her. We would have to get off. With some effort, I lowered the dog to the ground, got off and unhooked the cinch. My fingers were so cold, I could hardly make them work. I righted the saddle, but my arms were too weak to lift Hobbin again, and we were losing precious time. My dog lay on the ground with his ears down, looking miserable. There was blood everywhere. I screamed out, "Is there anyone there? Can anyone help me?!" No answer. Who would be there? It was 40 degrees and pouring down rain.

Utterly exhausted, I picked up the dog and started walking. I had heard about the strength people get from adrenaline in an emergency. I *should* be able to sling Hobbin over my shoulder and just walk out, I thought. But I couldn't do it. Setting him down, I started dragging him by his collar. Stop. Rest. Carry him a few steps. Stop. Rest. Drag him a bit farther.

I was terribly thirsty. I tried to drink the rain with little success. When I could, I drank the drops that dripped off the branches over the trail. I tried not to think about how far we had to go, or how hard this was on Hobbin. He would look at me, and I would tell him to just keep trying. And he did. Sometimes I would just hold up his front end, and he would do his best to "walk" his back legs. When he faltered, I dragged him. Two hours after the shooting, we made it to the highway.

If you have worked with young horses, you can appreciate what K'Pio had been experiencing during this time. In addition to the shooting and the yelling and the slipping saddle, she had not been ridden in the rain before. Now it was coming down hard, and we were standing beside the road with cars and trucks driving by, headlights on, spraying water and making different noises than they do on dry pavement. Still, she did fine.

We managed to get across the road and up the driveway to a nearby house. The lady who owned it, a woman in her 80s, had often spoken with me as I rode by. K'Pio got jumpy walking past all the stuff in the yard, but Hobbin picked up strength. He actually walked up on the porch and lay down. The owner came out, and I hurriedly told her my story, apologizing for the blood on the porch. Then I stood in the rain and held K'Pio as she dialed my house. My husband said he would come right away. I asked the woman for some water and waited.

Finally, my husband arrived. He loaded Hobbin into the van, and I got on my horse to ride home. It was then that K'Pio freaked out. Once Hobbin disappeared, she just fell apart. She shied at everything—the trucks on the road, the ditch, the noise my wet jeans made against the saddle. She pranced. She whinnied. She tried to take off. I didn't dare go faster than a walk. It took a long time to ride the mile and a half home.

The end of the story is quickly told. When I got to the house, I put K'Pio in the barn, and my husband drove us the 30 miles to the veterinarian, who said Hobbin would be treated for shock that night and x-rayed in the morning.

In the morning we learned the extent of Hobbin's injuries. The bullet had gone into the left side of his muzzle from above, shattering when it hit the dense upper jawbone. The pieces continued up through the sinuses and were stopped by the bone around the eye. The veterinarian decided to leave them in place, fearing it would only do more damage to operate. Hobbin might lose some teeth, he said, but his eye would be OK. I was filled with relief. All during the ordeal, I had been sure the eye was ruined.

We took Hobbin home and nursed him with antibiotics and soft food. One year later, he is still with us. And except for a few moments of hesitation when meeting strangers in the woods, he has returned to his normal, friendly self.

My wonderful horse was set back in her training for a while. When we went on the trail, K'Pio would watch Hobbin closely and nearly come to a stop if he disappeared for a moment. The sound of cars on wet pavement still makes her tense. But she continues to make progress.

My recovery has been the slowest of all. After the shooting, it was hard for me to go back to riding on the trail. I was watchful, and I listened for vehicles or voices. I bought a cellular phone to take with me. Some friends advised me to buy a gun, but each time I replayed the scene in my mind, I could not see it happening differently if I had been armed.

Still, I have not given up. I have many wonderful memories of riding in these woods. I have met mostly good people on the trail, and I have felt totally connected to nature. Even if that sense of peace returns only occasionally, I will go on riding. It may never be the way it was, but it is part of who I am.

LUCKY EDDY

*A horse owner's worst nightmare—a runaway
mare, lost in the mountains—turns out to
be a blessing in disguise.*

BY LISSA-MARIE WELCH

When I purchased my five-year-old Quarter Horse mare, I was sure she would make a great trail horse. At 14.3 hands, Eddy was just the right size to fit under tree limbs and get through narrow spots. She had good conformation, and I liked her looks, too—she was coal black, with a perfect heart shape marked in white on her forehead.

I started her out on the steep trails around our San Francisco Bay-area cattle ranch, and she quickly gained confidence on the narrow cow paths. Within two months, she was in excellent condition. I decided that the upcoming Memorial Day weekend would be the perfect time to take her up to the Sierra Nevada high country for some serious trail-riding practice.

This was my first long trip with Eddy, and the two of us made frequent stops on our way to the mountains—even staying overnight with friends in Lake Tahoe, at 5,000 feet, to prepare for the 6,000-foot elevation where we'd be riding the next day. We finally arrived on Saturday morning at an area of the Toiyabe National Forest called Blue Lakes, a beautiful trailhead where I had brought horses before.

I unloaded Eddy from the two-horse trailer and tied her while I set up camp. I was planning several trail-riding sessions over the course of the next couple of days to get her used to the new terrain. Once camp was in order, I saddled my horse for our first wilderness ride.

We started off slowly because of the elevation, and I took care to stop and evaluate Eddy's condition frequently as we rode. To my surprise, she handled the change in altitude and scenery with ease. She was a little scared when she saw her first patches of snow, but within a short time she was taking the trails like a champ. Even the deer we came across did not spook her, maybe because she was so used to cattle already. She seemed very much at home in the mountains and was enjoying herself, and I was feeling confident that I had made the perfect choice in a trail companion for years to come.

Then I noticed the clouds on the horizon. That time of year in the Sierra Nevada, it is quite common for a thunderstorm to appear out of nowhere. Big, black, billowing clouds sneak up the mountainside, and the next thing you know, you're drenched. I decided to head back to camp and evaluate the weather situation.

Down at the campsite, I tied Eddy to the back of the trailer and unsaddled her as I watched the big black clouds grow closer. I was thinking maybe we should just pack up and call it a weekend. I didn't want to push my horse too hard on her first trip, and she had done so well already. At that moment, the sky lit up as far as I could see with the most brilliant show of lightning.

Spooked, Eddy jerked back on the rope. I just had time to think, "I'll never get *that* knot untied!" when the bull snap broke. The mare fell back on her hindquarters for about a second. Then she was up, her tail in the air, running in circles around the truck and trailer.

With all the trail riding I have done, all the competitions I have won, that moment stands out as one I will never forget. Eddy paused just once in her frantic circling, and then turned and took off up the four-wheel-drive road that leads to a wilderness of 300,000 acres. I sat down, stunned, and watched her running as fast as she could go up the same trail where, just hours earlier, I had so carefully paced our riding.

She was gone. Long gone. I got up and started to panic. In all the years I had cared for horses—worrying about the proper shoes, the proper diet, the right tack—I had never thought about losing one. Eddy's full name is *Ya we nodes eddy*, which is Apache for "she whose voice rides the wind." I kept thinking, "It's OK if you run around the ranch with your tail in the air, whinnying to your heart's content, but not here."

When I came to my senses, I drove to the nearest ranger station and reported my horse missing. I talked with the ranger for quite a while, and he recommended that I leave some feed at the site where I last saw her. As I put the alfalfa on the ground, I looked around at the rich green grass and the clear flowing streams and felt a positive flow of energy. Eddy would be fine up here until I could go home, get more horses and riders and come back to start a search.

The drive home from Blue Lakes takes about four hours. As the miles went by and reality took hold, I started to cry. My horse was up there all by herself. Anything might get her—mountain lions, bears, maybe people who would steal her and sell her for slaughter. I kept trying to think positively and keep a clear head, planning my return to find her. She is tough, and she'd adapted so well in such a short time, I thought. But I could not fool myself. Oh, I should never have taken that horse up there! I was just inside the Sacramento city limits when the cab of my Chevy Silverado suddenly filled with black smoke. It was hard to see, but I managed to put on my blinker and pull across the lanes to the side of the road. As I set the emergency brake, a man ran up and pulled me out of the truck, yelling, "Run! It's gonna blow!" He had been following me and had seen flames coming out under the engine.

The truck was quickly engulfed in fire. Thick smoke was everywhere, and Highway 50 shut down immediately. The next thing I knew, police officers and truck drivers were standing around me, shouting, "Are there horses in there?" The trailer has no windows, so they were unable to see inside.

Still in a state of shock, I told them, "No. I lost her."

"Not yet!" they yelled. "We'll save her."

"Wait," I said. "You don't understand—I *lost* her!"

Here were these wonderful people who were trying to help me, who were in such danger themselves, and I could not even convey to them that there were no horses in the trailer. I heard one man shout, "It's unhooked!" Then I realized that they had unhitched the trailer, and we were on an incline.

The trailer started rolling backwards toward a patrol car parked about 40 feet behind it. Frantically, we grabbed anything and everything on the side of the highway, trying to block the wheels. We got it stopped just in time, and the highway patrolman turned to me and grinned. "Darn!" he said. "That trailer must weigh 2,500 pounds. I almost had a new patrol car."

When the fire reached the gas tank, the truck really did blow. Thank God, everyone was clear. After the explosion, we just stood and watched it burn itself out. The man who had pulled me out of the cab came over and said, "Well, it doesn't look like much else can happen to you tonight, and I gotta go. I was already late getting home when this happened, and my wife is *never* going to believe this story."

After the fire was out, a fireman told me that it was caused by the fuel injection line, which had come loose and sprayed fuel over the hot engine. What saved me from smoke inhalation or burn injury, he said, was my habit of hauling with the window down and the doors unlocked—and, of course, that nice guy who pulled me out of the truck.

The next day, my husband and I called the Alpine County Sheriff's Department to ask about organizing a search party. They told us that we should probably hold off for a while, since we weren't familiar with the country and might get into trouble ourselves. The officials advised us to allow people who were already in the area—fire spotters, hunters, mountain climbers and the like—to keep an eye out for Eddy. We could come up to help if someone spotted her and we had a defined location to search. They also brought home to us the reality of the wilderness, with its wild predators and rough conditions. They had had reports of lost horses in the past, the deputies said, but usually the outcome was not favorable.

Still, I didn't give up. I kept calling everyone I could think of. I even got hold of the Alpine County telephone exchange and called randomly in the area to let local landowners know about my lost horse. I asked everyone to please contact the sheriff's department if they had a sighting.

Two and a half months went by. I purchased a new four-wheel-drive truck, but no one contacted me from Alpine County, and I gave up calling to check. I even talked to the horse broker who had sold me Eddy (and a gelding before her) to ask him to start looking for another horse. He encouraged me to move on, saying that domesticated horses these days just don't have it in them to survive the rough elements of the wilderness. Still, I found it hard to give up and say, "She's gone."

Then, one morning, while I was having breakfast, the telephone rang. It was Elaine Klavon from the Alpine County Search and Rescue. They had a sighting of a horse—a black horse wearing a red halter. That had to be Eddy.

I was so excited, I didn't even consider the person on the other end of the phone. I just started screaming and crying at the same time, right into the receiver. I couldn't believe that someone was really calling to tell me that Eddy had been seen.

Elaine explained that a deer hunter scouting the area before the season opened had called to report seeing a horse at 10,024 feet on Hawkins Peak, one of the highest mountains around. Ten thousand feet! Airplanes fly that high, I thought. The problem was, Elaine continued, that few potential rescuers were willing to take a horse up that high. She would call me back if she could round up a group of volunteers.

Luck was on our side. Two local endurance riders, Gary and Kathy Ceragioli, not only offered to help with the search but said they would provide horses for two additional riders. Sheriff's department 911 dispatcher Chris Branscombe called a friend, Paula Cotter, and the two women joined the party. All four were experienced Search and Rescue team members, although this was not an official assignment. A local rancher, Roy Hatcher, said he would drive a trailer up as far as he could to pick up the lost horse if they found her. The group headed to the highest trailhead they could reach; it would be a three-hour ride from there to the top of the mountain.

Just before the searchers headed out, Elaine phoned to let me know they had gotten the volunteers together and would call that night with results. It was the longest day of my life. I had so many mixed emotions: What would Eddy's condition be, mentally and physically? Would they even be able to catch her?

I could picture the nice quiet ride in the crisp mountain air. That's just the kind of experience that keeps me coming back to Toiyabe National Forest. I truly wished I was up there riding with them, although I knew that having me along was the last thing they wanted or needed. These were professionals, trained to handle many different situations, but they didn't know what they would have to deal with when they found the mare—*if* they could find her.

The rescuers rode all the way up Hawkins Peak, Elaine told me later, and there she was. They found Eddy next to a pond, with lush green grass and the best view around. Friendly horse that she is, she just walked right up to them. She still had her red halter on, but her hooves were worn so badly that she was limping. Slowly, they ponied her down the mountain to where the trailer was waiting. Eddy climbed right on, and they hauled her to Roy's ranch and put her up for the night in the barn.

My husband and I drove up the very next day. I will never forget the look on Eddy's face. She had her ears up, and she whinnied at me, as if to say, "I want to go home, Mom!" She looked great, considering her experience. Apart from the sore hooves, she had only a few scratches from running in the brush and a bump on her nose from the halter.

After thanking everyone for their efforts and kindness, we took Eddy home. Amazingly, she suffered no long-term effects from her ordeal. Her feet healed fine, and a few weeks' work with a trainer restored her old confident personality.

Maybe things do happen for a reason. As terrifying as it was to lose my horse, I know that she would never have lived through the truck fire and explosion, and I thank God she was not in the trailer when it happened. When I first picked Eddy for her conformation, I didn't know that it would be something I couldn't see—her spirit and heart—that would make the difference in her survival.

Spirit and heart were plentiful, too, in the people who are part of this story. If it were not for the hunter who took the time to call and report seeing her, and the rescuers who volunteered their horses, time and expertise, I would not be enjoying my Eddy today. I would still have a piece of my life missing somewhere in the mountains. And if it were not for the brave act of the stranger who pulled me from my truck, I would not be here myself. Tears come to my eyes as I think about the unselfish, kind people who helped us.

Eddy and I thank you.

A MUDTIME STORY

*A horse's trust in her owner brings a happy ending
to a sticky springtime adventure.*

BY MIKE LEVISON

Calamities happened daily that spring in southern California. For weeks, we'd been glued to our TV sets, watching rivers of mud flow down quiet residential streets. We'd seen mountains collapsing and large, beautiful homes being swept off their foundations. Landslides blocked highways and railroads, and dry creeks had become raging rivers. From Laguna Beach north to Malibu and up the coast to Santa Barbara, cars were buried up to their windows in mud. There were power failures everywhere. Most of a beachfront mobile home park near Ventura had been washed out to sea. It was a typical spring.

Finally, near the end of March, the rain stopped. The skies cleared and turned crystal blue. The air in the Santa Clarita Valley was scrubbed so clean we could count the pine trees on mountain ridges 10 miles away. The temperature was back up in the 70s. I felt grateful—and a little smug—for having been spared the calamities so common to our region. After more than a week of rain, it was a "good to be alive" day. I couldn't wait to get out for a relaxing trail ride.

My wife, Ruthann, and I are fortunate that our home in

Sand Canyon is adjacent to the Angeles National Forest. There are also several large movie ranches and parcels of undeveloped private land accessible to local riders. The terrain is grassy meadows scattered with 200-year-old oak trees, and rolling foothills that merge with rugged mountains climbing to more than 4,000 feet. Many of Hollywood's Western movies have been filmed in our immediate locale.

The day was so spectacular, it was easy to convince Ruthann that the trails would not be too muddy or spongy for her to join me on the ride. Eagerly, we groomed our three horses: Spotlite, the home-bred, six-year-old Morab pinto mare who runs loose with us when not ridden; Serby, Ruthann's 16-year-old chestnut Arabian gelding; and Marita, my stocky, 14-year-old chestnut Morgan mare.

I fondly recall the day we were shopping for horses 11 years ago. We had found a Morgan breeder with a shedrow full of well-broken horses for sale. I looked across the parking area to see eight horses' heads hanging over the Dutch doors, watching us with idle curiosity. Locking eyes with the second from the right, I walked to her as if magnetized, holding out my cupped hand. She never broke eye contact as she sniffed and licked the back of my hand and stole my heart forever.

Fortunately for me, Marita was very well schooled. She possessed a marshmallow-soft jog, would stop instantly on a spoken "whoa," neck-reined almost by telepathy and was beautiful to look at as well. I would have bought that horse with only three legs. With some justification, Ruthann has often told our friends that if we were ever to divorce, she would name Marita as corespondent.

Still, I must reluctantly admit that my horse is not perfect. She will not tolerate crossties or being snubbed short. (However, she will ground-tie like a statue.) When confronted suddenly with wet spots on a trail, she will either commence a Ginger Rogers tap-dance routine or imitate Pegasus, the flying horse. She thinks quick, backward steps will produce wings as she prepares to lift off. But if the ground is firm, Marita will go anywhere I ask.

We left our barn around 2 p.m., five happy creatures strolling through brilliant sunshine, heading for our favorite six-mile loop. We crossed meadows full of wildflowers and bright-green new grass, much to Spotlite's delight. She munched her way along, the world her smorgasbord, always keeping us within sight.

As we headed up into the hills, the trail footing was reasonably firm, but off the trail the horses would sink six or eight inches into the saturated earth. Marita, customarily in the lead, needed no encouragement to stay centered on the firm paths. We climbed our familiar foothills, occasionally pausing to marvel at the spectacular 50-mile panoramic views from the high ridges. The beauty of the day, combined with the companionship of our horses, filled us with a sense of contentment.

On our descent back into Sand Canyon, we came upon a deep, water-carved, four-foot-wide gully. The only alternative to jumping this chasm was to ride down into the ravine that ran alongside the trail. Marita did not recognize a Pegasus moment when I needed one, so we descended cautiously into the heavy chaparral and sagebrush, trailblazing our way to circumvent the washout. Working our way downward, we arrived at an open flat area about 40 feet in diameter. Ruthann, on Serby, and Spotlite were a dozen yards behind us.

Water trickled gently along the edge of the flat area. Sprouts of young grass grew in the coarse, sandy surface. Surrounding the flat there was a natural-looking six-foot berm, and beyond it a familiar dirt road. This combination of factors led me to assume firm ground, and Marita seemed in accord. (Later, I would learn it was a newly excavated catch basin, dug in an effort to control the heavy mud runoff from the hills.)

We started across, traveled about 10 feet and stopped. Marita had sunk in up to her knees! Surprisingly, she did not panic. I was about to apologize for getting her into yet another fine mess when my stirrups touched the mud. Under the circumstances, a fast dismount seemed a good idea.

As I stood alongside the mare, we both continued to sink. I glanced over my shoulder to see the rest of our entourage watching, frozen, from the firm side of the berm. Three pairs of eyes were saucer-wide. Astonishment and disbelief were written on their faces. As the mud reached my armpits, I vividly recalled the scene in the old Tarzan film: A hunter steps into quicksand and starts sinking out of sight, desperately waving one futile hand. I thought, "What an awful and unexpected way to go, and how terrible to be taking my beloved horse with me!"

Fortunately, just as the mud reached the top of my shoulders and covered Marita's back, only two inches short of her withers, we stopped sinking. Ruthann, highly distressed but finally able to speak, asked, "What should I do?" I told her to find a phone and call 911. Reluctantly, she took off, with Spotlite trailing behind.

The mud was about the consistency of pancake batter, and I found that, by sort of lying on it, I was able to maneuver about. My fear of immediate drowning was gone now that I knew the basin was only five feet deep. But concern for Marita was a different matter. I reached down into the mud and unfastened the cinch so I could remove my saddle and blanket. Growing more confident in my ability to move around, I carried them near the berm and tossed them onto dry ground.

When I carried the saddle away, Marita thought I was leaving her. She gave a leap, and I saw she had moved forward about four inches with the effort. I prayed that this would be the solution to our predicament. Then I realized that my reins were out of sight. The last thing we needed was for them to tangle around Marita's front legs. That would pull her head down into the mud, with disastrous consequences. I quickly removed the bridle and recovered the reins.

As I pulled off the headstall, Marita leaped two more times, traveling about four inches each time. I could see, however, that her head was dropping closer to the mud with each effort. The exertion required to both leap and hold her head out of the mud was quickly exhausting her. She would probably drown before covering the few yards to safety.

I moved in front of her, took her chin in my hand and lifted her head. As I held her, she relaxed and rested. After a minute or so, I looped the loose reins around her neck. Giving a tug, I told her to jump. She did, and moved forward another few inches. Slowly, we repeated the procedure over and over, with me holding her chin in my hand for brief rest periods between leaps. The result was slow but steady progress. To my amazement, during the entire ordeal neither fear nor panic ever appeared in her large, intelligent eyes.

A traumatic and exhausting half hour later, we scrambled up the berm together. Marita looked like "The Creature from the Black Lagoon," and I looked even worse! She gave a huge shake in an effort to dislodge the thick layer of mud that clung to her. Then she began nibbling on the sweet green sprouts growing along the side of the dirt road. I knew all was well.

As I followed Marita up the berm, I could see a fire captain's car driving up Cambria Road toward us. A large fire truck was right behind it. Trotting along behind them were two horses and one rider. Swallowing a laugh, I watched the expression on the captain's face change instantly from grim anxiety to immense relief. The two sorry, mud-covered creatures he saw meant that he need not perform a difficult rescue. No expensive helicopter with a horse sling would be required. There would be no tragic outcome to explain; no TV news crews to deal with. He relaxed visibly as he greeted us and made sure we were all right.

Later, back at home, it took Ruthann more than an hour with a garden hose to wash the sticky mud off me, Marita and the saddle. As I submitted to the hosing, I proudly reflected on my forbearance with the fire captain. Though it was the perfect opportunity, I thought, I never once gave in to the temptation to tell him, "I did all I could, but I just wasn't able to save the other horse and rider!"

INKY'S HIJINKS

A pony's mischievous nature gets him into trouble,
but his sensible temperament makes rescuing
him a little easier.

BY FAYE W. LITTLE

"The party owning a green, two-horse trailer with a black pony in it should go to their trailer immediately." The words coming over the public address at the horse show seemed extremely loud, but maybe that's just because I knew they were directed toward me. Panic stricken, I raced back to the parking lot.

It was a beautiful Saturday, and my 10-year-old daughter, Brooke, and I had loaded up her two ponies for a day of horse-show experience. When the announcement was made, I was watching her in the schooling ring with Birchwood, a 4-year-old gray Welsh pony.

Birchwood was a promising show prospect, but Inky, whom we'd left back at the trailer, was Brooke's *special,* all-around-fun pony. Inky was the pony she spent her afternoons with at our Thoroughbred farm, galloping about with no saddle and usually only some baling twine for a bridle. Inky was the pony with whom Brooke played hide-and-seek with neighborhood riders, and it was Inky who loved jumping anything he and Brooke could find. The two of them amazed our trainer by treating the loading ramp we use for horses at the farm like a bank jump. Inky even let the family dogs ride with Brooke. And although Inky seemed to be about as wide as he was tall, he still won his fair share of ribbons in both hunter and Western classes, and he had even won two pony races.

Today, when last we'd seen him, Inky had been standing in the trailer with a full hay net, munching contentedly.

I was expecting trouble, but when I got back to the parking area, I found I was unprepared for what I found. Inky was always inclined for mischievous stunts. If a gate was open or a barn broom had been eaten, we always knew to look for Inky. This time, however, his sense of adventure had gotten him into real danger.

Apparently, Inky had decided he'd eaten enough hay and resented being left alone in the trailer while all his friends were at the schooling ring. He'd tried to jump the four-foot chest bar, and there he hung. His halter was still tied with a flexible rubber strap, which twisted and pulled his head back into a terribly awkward position. Inky looked like a heap of black fur nearly standing on his head by the escape door. His eyes were tightly closed, and there was no movement to indicate that he was breathing. I was sure his neck was broken.

Not a person was near our trailer when I arrived. Whoever turned in the emergency announcement to the horse-show office had left, and Brooke was still back at the ring with Birchwood. How could I get Inky out of the trailer alone?

I rarely carry a pocketknife, much to my husband's annoyance, but today, just by chance, I happened to have a small one in my pocket. I used it to cut the rubber tie, and Inky's head fell to the floor with a loud thump. To my great relief, I saw his eye blink. He was alive, at least. But he made no effort to struggle. Either he was terribly injured—from the position he was in any bone in his body could have been broken—or he knew he was in a fix and was waiting for someone to get him out. (Did I mention Inky is also *very* intelligent?)

Inky's hind legs were hanging over the chest bar, and there was no way I could release it while it supported all of his weight. The only solution I could see was to open the escape door; with any luck, maybe I'd find the strength to push his rear end over the bar and out the door.

Brooke came back about then. I hadn't wanted her to see her beloved pony in such danger, but to my surprise, she was a real trouper—no tears, just a very helpful attitude. Brooke opened the escape door, and with all my strength I was able to push Inky's legs over and off of the chest bar. As I'd hoped, his hindquarters rotated over and fell through the door and onto the ground outside. But we still had to pull his front end out of the trailer; this meant rolling his front legs up so we could position him to get him through the door. Soon we were able to pull his front half out onto the ground. Of course, his head and neck landed right under the corner of the door. I had visions of him suddenly beginning to struggle and slicing his head or neck on the sharp metal edge, but we couldn't close the door without moving him first. With Brooke tugging on his halter and another lady and me pulling on his mane and front legs, we were able to slide him out of danger, and Brooke quickly closed the door.

Inky had no outward injuries—no cuts or blood—but we still didn't know how badly he might have been hurt. It had been fortunate that he had never fussed or struggled while we were moving him—there were many moments I would have been in an unsafe position had he thrashed or kicked. Now, his eyes were open and he was breathing, but he continued to lie still.

After several minutes with no movement, I gave him a little tap with my boot and said, "Get up, Inky. You are OK." It seemed to be what he was waiting to hear. Slowly but surely, he got to his feet and gave a big shake to remove the dirt and hay from his haircoat. Brooke walked him around, carefully watching each step. He was fine. We all gave a sigh of relief.

Brooke and I decided we'd had enough excitement for one day, so we loaded the ponies and headed for home. Amazingly, Inky had no fear of returning to the trailer; he followed Brooke straight up the ramp and began eating hay as if nothing unusual had happened. Brooke was sure he was being contrite because he realized his problems were all his own fault. We also expected him to be a bit sore, but the next day Brooke rode him around the farm, and he moved as easily as ever.

We'd hoped Inky had learned his lesson, but we were careful to avoid leaving him in the trailer alone again. Yet that wasn't the end of his pranks. Years later, we parked the trailer while we had dinner during a long-distance haul, leaving Inky inside with a Thoroughbred mare. Our mistake that time was leaving a bale of hay and half a bag of feed covered in plastic in the front of the trailer. We thought there was *no* way Inky could reach the feed while tied. Wrong. When we got back, Inky was still tied, chest bar in place, quietly munching on the hay in his hay net. However, the plastic cover, feed bag and extra hay were in the center of the trailer, with both animals proudly standing on everything. Normally, the plastic would have scared the mare, but with Inky at her side she was enjoying the prank. We had to unload both and repack before we could continue our trip.

Inky tried our patience many times, but it was hard to get mad at him. He always seemed to have a grin on his face that made us smile with him. He was a wonderful member of our family and Brooke's best friend for 22 years.

CHAPTER 3

COMFORT AND JOY

FRIEND FOR LIFE

As a young girl comes of age and pursues her dreams, her childhood mount proves to be the horse of a lifetime.

BY CHARMIAN WRIGHT, DVM

Last year I went for a summer afternoon ride to enjoy the softening colors of the waning day along the foothills. Cantering toward home, my Appaloosa-Arabian, full of himself, seemed ready to go four directions at once. I laughed, feeling his strength and energy, gripping his bare sides with my legs. I loved to see him that way—proud and happy and full of life.

Almost home, we caught up with two people I knew walking on the side of the road, and I pulled up to say hello. Boo tossed his head at the delay, dancing forward and side-passing in the road. They ducked out of his way. "You'd better train that horse for an endurance ride," one of them said, laughing. "Calm him down a little!" As if in response, Boo began to paw at the asphalt stiff-leggedly, sending sparks flying into the dimming evening light.

"Naw," I said, raising my voice over the clattering hooves. "He's 29 years old."

I was just 10, with all of four years of riding experience behind me, when my family purchased the 2-year-old gelding named Boo. Something about that little red spotted horse had caught my youthful heart; he was lean, tough, strong and very, very fast.

Together, he and I shared all the things horsey kids do. I rode almost constantly back then, before school, after school, sometimes during school. I brought Boo into the house a few times, took him on picnics, practiced riding standing up, read horse books while lying on his back. We spent many long hours and days and years playing and racing through streams and over mountains around my house.

I joined 4-H, and we competed in barrels, trail, pleasure, pole bending. Boo won many ribbons, as all the horses in 4-H do. But he was best in the costume classes, outfitted as an Indian pony. With his wild black mane and wiry Appaloosa looks, dressed in sheepskins and eagle feathers, and running with only a leather thong around his jaw, he always seemed to catch the judge's eye.

He was also an extraordinary jumper, able to clear well over five feet as a 4-year-old. I had no one to tell me this was too high—not that I would have listened. I was thrilled to be flying through the air, surging with the feeling that my horse could do anything.

As a teenager, I discovered horse camping. My friends and I would ride through the Wasatch Mountains for days at a time, exploring miles of little-used trails. Boo was clever and confident in the high country, able to negotiate even the toughest terrain, and I trusted him implicitly. During one high-school summer, Boo and I spent a month alone in the Uinta Mountains, accompanied only by my dog and a pack donkey. On Highline Trail, we reached Dead Horse Pass, a treacherous, aptly named descent. From the vaulted height at the top of the pass, I eyed the long, narrow, broken path below, with its steep sides of loose scree sliding down among ragged, vertical cliffs. Whole pack strings had reportedly slid off that precarious trail and over the cliffs to their deaths. But going around the pass would mean a roundabout trip of 20 or 30 extra miles.

Despite my misgivings, I started leading Boo down the trail, leaving the donkey tied at the top, awaiting his turn. After a few strides Boo stopped dead, refusing to take another step. Carefully I climbed onto his back and willed him to go on, as I did when we galloped toward a jump. That was all he needed to bolster his confidence. I sat very still as he negotiated his way downward, his nose low and ears intent, as if he was carefully planning every delicate step. Even the ring of the lonely donkey's bray echoing from the cliffs above did not distract him; he swiveled his eyes up the hill only briefly before carrying me safely all the way to the bottom.

When my time came to leave home—to enter the preveterinary program at Utah State University in Logan—Boo came with me. The idea of selling him or leaving him behind was just unthinkable. Despite the poverty of student life, I always scrimped enough to keep my horse. And I'm glad I did, because throughout those difficult years, Boo was a vital reminder of the goals I was working toward and a link to the life I had grown to love.

Many students develop fond memories of life in the dorms, campus parties and activities, and life in a college town. I have those memories, too, but I also fondly recall galloping along the farm roads at sunset, climbing high mountain trails, riding between green and golden waves of barley and field corn, and watching the horses play in glittering new snow.

After Utah State I went to Colorado State University for veterinary school, and Boo came along. Classes were demanding and studying consumed much of my time, leaving little left for riding. But what time I did spend with Boo—brushing and feeding him, and taking him on short rides—was a welcome solace. And Boo helped me to appreciate anatomy. In our first year, my classmates and I memorized every dip and ridge on every bone in dogs, cats and horses. We learned about every muscle, its origin and insertions, its action, its connecting tendons and ligaments. While riding, I began to feel and visualize the strong, smooth interplay of Boo's muscles at the canter, feel the orchestration of limbs as his hooves struck the ground with a precisely ordered balance and sequence. Feeling his heart beating with my left heel, I could envision the intricate, powerful flow of blood through complex vascular networks. Later, the knowledge and understanding of living things was to become second nature. But at that time, the learning, although difficult and complicated, was in many ways magical.

By the time I graduated from veterinary school, I'd had Boo for 18 years. He had helped me navigate the difficult terrain of childhood, adolescence and adulthood. In the midst of change, he had been a constant source of stability, my tie to the land, and my link to adventure. But now the long years of college were finally over.

After years of study, having time to ride again was like rediscovering a long-lost gift. I moved back to Utah and opened my own equine veterinary practice, and finally I was living my own life once again, working in a profession that I loved. In my time off I would take Boo up Red Pine canyon, where golden aspen leaves drifted lazily across the ground in the soft, dappled sunlight, or gallop him down a secret mountain trail, his hoofbeats resonating in the forest silence.

In the autumn of 1991 Boo participated in the next milestone of my life, when I married Gordon Croissant in a horseback ceremony atop Flagstaff Peak. We approached the guests from either side of the peak; Gordon on his big Belgian took the dirt road to the north, while Boo and I rode around the trackless south side. Never before had Boo worn a sidesaddle, nor I a wedding dress, and the steep ground was rocky and tangled with shrubs. However, autumn had cloaked the mountains in a kind of glory, and my horse carried me with confidence and ease. Before we came into sight of the wedding party, we had a few moments to ourselves, Boo and I, and I thought about the many times when as a child I had ridden Boo on the western slopes of these very mountains, and falling away in the mists to the east I could just make out the Uintas. As we rounded a corner to face the guests, a breeze caught the train of my dress and the horse's long tail, and the guests fell suddenly silent. My heart was singing as my father came forward to lead me the final distance into my new life.

In the years since then our adventures have continued. Boo and I have thoroughly explored the canyons around our home. We have ridden in Nevada's Valley of Fire and around the shores of Lake Mead. We have galloped in the broad, beautiful valleys of the West Desert and raced antelope on the rim of Cottonwood Wash. We have returned to the Uintas and cantered in those high green meadows that seem to touch the sky, looking out over the trails we had ridden, alone together, 20 years and a lifetime ago.

Boo is now approaching 30, and we have been together 28 years. He still prances and jumps, and he bucks on command. Although his endurance is not what it was, he will break into a dead run at an unspoken signal, and he can cling to the side of a mountain like no other horse I have known. He still fights to get to the front of the pack and will search out a trail on the darkest night. He loves to play in the snowy down with his girlfriend, a young chestnut mare; he snakes his neck at her and crowhops to her side, then stands with head high to snort at the rising sun.

Thinking back on all my years with Boo brings me joy—but also a few tears, because I know that no horse can live forever. But for now, each day that we spend together is a gift. And as we gallop home, he stretches his head forward, hooves flying; I lean over his withers, grinning, carried into the face of the wind.

THE MOST PATIENT TEACHER

*A seemingly ordinary polo pony caught a
young woman's eye, captured her heart
and left behind a legacy of love.*

BY DEIDRE SHARP

"You need to learn to love higher up on the food chain," a
prospective boyfriend once told me, after I had chosen to ride my
horse in a snowstorm rather than go out to dinner with him. He
and I never made it beyond a few dates, but that horse, Rasta, and
I were together for 14 wonderful years. And, looking back, the pain
of losing him was stronger than the loss of any boyfriend.

I remember the first time I saw Rasta. I was working as a
groom and trainer for an Argentinean polo player based in
Portsmouth, Rhode Island. Rasta had just arrived on a truck with
several other prospects, and he was not a horse who would catch
many second glances. The scrawny little appendix Quarter Horse
gelding was about a hundred pounds underweight, and his scruffy
bay coat was half shed out. At 15.1 hands, he was just the right size
for polo; however, he quickly earned himself the unaffectionate
nickname "No Brakes" because he would not stop when asked.

As a member of the polo club, I was required to take one lesson per week. One day, when it was time for my lesson, all of the
horses were either on rest or waiting in reserve to play that after-

noon, and the only horse available was No Brakes. I figured that since the lesson was in the arena and it would probably be slow-paced, I could manage him, so I tacked him up and got on.

Much to my surprise, he responded beautifully. He was wonderful in the walk, trot and canter, he neck-reined well, and I had no problems stopping him whenever I asked. After the lesson, I washed him down and examined him more closely. He had a short back and clean legs. His chest was wide and his girth deep, with plenty of room for heart and lung. I looked at his face—the broad forehead and big wide eyes. What got me were those eyes. I saw trust, honesty and friendship. Immediately and without thinking about it, I walked over to the barn manager to negotiate buying him. "How strange," I thought. "Why am I doing this?" The answer was simple. "It's the right thing to do."

No Brakes was nothing at all like the big, dark-gray Irish Thoroughbred I had always pictured myself buying someday. I had ridden jumpers in Virginia and Maryland from childhood through my late teens, but I gave it up when a horse I had shown for five years—and brought along to champion status—was sold out from under me. Not long after that, I left the horse world to go sailing in the Caribbean. Seven years later, after one storm too many, I found myself in Rhode Island, and the dry land felt good under my feet. Soon I was looking for a way to get involved with horses again, and now here I was buying my first horse.

The first thing I did was change his name to Rasta. For a young horse, he was very mellow, like the Rastafarians I had known in the Caribbean. In two days he knew the sound of my voice, and in less than two weeks he knew the sight and sound of my car. Granted, I was his "food person," but I also felt that a strong understanding was rapidly forming between us. *This* horse would never be "sold out from under me."

Rasta quickly learned to play polo, but we also enjoyed many other sports together. We jumped, we did team penning, reining and second-level dressage. But trail rides were his favorites, along with swimming in the ocean. Often, he was my patient teacher, and even a baby-sitter at times; I sometimes felt I needed his help more than he needed mine.

I always thought he was a pretty good judge of human character. Although he was usually easy to handle, on one occasion he wouldn't let a certain farrier come near him. Rasta seemed terrified of him. Shortly after that, the man suddenly left the area, and it was discovered that he had scammed and stolen from a lot of local people. Somehow, I think Rasta knew the man was a criminal.

For nine years Rasta and I grew together. During the tenth year I acquired two Thoroughbred mares. Rasta liked having his own herd, and the three horses became friends. The mares followed Rasta's example, becoming relaxed and gentle. The four of us settled into a comfortable routine of ring work, trail rides and lots of quiet handling.

But our lives changed forever the day in October 1998 when Rasta came up lame in his right front leg. It was very sudden. The night before he was perfectly fine, but the next morning he could barely set his hoof down. Given the degree of lameness, I thought it very odd that I could find no heat, swelling or outward signs of trauma. But he was eating, and he seemed quite happy except for his sore foot. I hoped it was a stone bruise, but just for my peace of mind, I called the veterinarian.

When E.J. Finocchio, DVM, picked up Rasta's foot, he found a puncture wound. The spongy texture of the frog had caused the wound to cover over, and I had missed it completely. The situation did not look good; a deep infection was likely, and the location of the wound could involve tendons and bones. The veterinarian set to work opening and flushing the wound, but he also recommended that Rasta be hospitalized, so he could receive intravenous antibiotics and his condition would be closely monitored.

The next day I took Rasta to the New England Horse Care Center. In the ordeal that followed, Finocchio as well as Edna Currid, MVB, and Scott Marshall, DVM, would be my heroes, guides and mentors in the struggle to save my horse.

Rasta's spirits never flagged. He settled right in at the hospital, even dunking his hay in his water bucket, just like he did at home. For several days he seemed to improve, but on the fourth day, he took a turn for the worse. Currid, choosing a more aggressive treatment, decided to operate in order to thoroughly debride the affected area and also infuse it with antibiotics. The infection had reached the bursa and tendon sheaths around the small bones inside the hoof. Ten days later, with the infection returning, Rasta had to undergo the procedure again. Through all of this, Rasta's appetite remained strong, and he always seemed happy to see me, so it was hard for me to comprehend how serious his wound really was.

Finally, after two weeks, I was able to bring Rasta home, where I hand-walked him twice a day. But when Finocchio stopped by a week later, he said he was concerned about the way Rasta was using his foot. He feared a bone infection and the possibility that adhesions—scar tissue from the inflammation—were fusing one or more bones or tendons within his pastern. The pain was causing Rasta to hold his foot up, and this, in turn, was causing his tendons to contract; unless we could reverse that scarring and contraction, Rasta's foot would be permanently locked in that bent position.

After X rays confirmed Finocchio's fears, we added extensive stretching exercises to Rasta's twice-daily workout. Our hope was that the stretches could counteract the tendon contraction and straighten his foot. But it would be a difficult struggle. The week before Christmas, Currid stopped by and gave Rasta a nerve block, which enabled him to stand with his foot flat on the ground. At last, it seemed, there was hope that we'd be able to make progress.

But the optimism was guarded at best. Over the next few months, Rasta would seem to progress, putting his foot down consistently, only to experience setback after setback. Whenever they were in the neighborhood, all three veterinarians would make unscheduled stops at my barn. Even on Rasta's bad days, though, there always seemed to be some hope that he would recover.

In February, Finocchio and Marshall examined Rasta. He was improving a bit again, and we decided to try another operation. This time, they would sever his contracted tendon along with a couple of the nerves that go to his foot. The goal was to enable him to stand and walk with his foot flat on the ground, even though he'd never be able to carry a rider. That didn't matter. I wanted him to hang out with the mares, eat grass and be a horse. I just wanted him to live.

This surgery went well, and Rasta came home a week later to resume our routine of stretching and hand-walking. Currid and I created a brace to give the leg some support. Again, Rasta seemed to improve but not for long.

Spring arrived warm and beautiful. All around us, life was responding to the new season, but in my barn, hope for Rasta was fading. Due to wear from the brace, the skin on his fetlock joint was started to break down, and our exercises were losing their impact. Despite our best efforts, the fetlock joint appeared to be fusing in a bent position. I called Finocchio, who advised me to remove the brace and schedule another examination. I made the appointment for a few days later. Over those days, I did a lot of thinking and even more crying.

It was a gorgeous day, bright and breezy, when Finocchio arrived. After he saw Rasta, we both knew what needed to be done. I never thought I could do it, but I had to. I felt a hurt beyond any

I had ever felt in my life. A short time later, we set Rasta's spirit free to run with the May winds.

I believe in the sacredness of all life and that all paths are to be honored. I feel that all creatures can teach us and help guide us through life. Rasta was a great teacher. He showed me the importance of trust and the power of unconditional love. He never cared what I looked like or how much money I had. His was the strong shoulder I could always lean on. He was always positive and eager to please. He was kind and gentle. Perhaps most important, he taught me forgiveness. He forgave my mistakes. He forgave my occasional outbursts of anger and frustration. He forgave my ego. He was my best friend.

I let him go while he was still happy, before his condition worsened, and that's how I will always remember him. And I will try to take the lessons I learned from him and share them with others. For now, though, I am looking to my mares to help guide me.

MY EYES FOR HIS FEET

She needed his legs; he needed her eyes. Together they learned how to conquer their limitations.

BY INA MAE BROOKS

One fall afternoon when the sumac was a blaze of crimson and the air was so fresh and crisp I could not stay inside, I decided to take my new horse—my first—for a ride. Trigger, a beautiful paint, was at the far side of the pasture.

When I whistled, he lifted his head, turned and twitched his ears. I whistled again, but he would not come. So I headed across the field, dragging the heavy saddle with me. The bridle flopped on my shoulder, and my pockets bulged with corn. Trigger stood in the distance, head high and ears erect. As I came near him, my ankle twisted and I fell, but I got up and limped on. Polio had paralyzed my legs when I was a child, but I had recovered enough to walk and, despite my weak muscles, I hoped to roam the countryside on Trigger's back. A spoiled, headstrong 13-year-old, I was too impatient to allow for limitations, especially my own.

My left leg was the weakest, and I was unable to use that knee to climb onto a horse, but Trigger was gentle enough for me to mount from the right side. First I had to catch him; he had turned and walked away. With a sigh, I dropped the saddle and followed him to a corner where the fences crossed.

After I caught up with him, I grabbed the rope halter and put the bridle over his ears. "Here, have some grain," I said and thrust some under his nose. When he opened his mouth for the food, I slipped the bit between his teeth. "*Good* boy!" I positioned the bridle and buckled the straps. Reins in hand, I led him along the fence to where I'd left the saddle. When we stopped, I said to him, "I know I can saddle you, but can I mount you out here?" I had never done that. "If I'm ever going to ride," I said, "I have to learn how to get on your back no matter where we are."

"Don't let your horse step away when you mount," Dad had warned. "His left side has to be against a barrier. Remember, if he sidesteps you can't hop on that left foot like other girls."

With Trigger's side against the fence, I threw the blanket on his back and swung the saddle into place. I reached under his belly, grabbed the strap and cinched it. With the reins wrapped around the saddle horn, I thrust my right foot into the stirrup. With my right hand, I grabbed his mane and with my left took the reins and used the saddle horn to pull myself up. However, the saddle slowly slid around until I clung to it upside down beneath Trigger's belly. Plop! I landed on my back in fresh manure. Trigger shifted and stepped around me with his head pulled downward, because I still held the reins.

"You *stupid* beast!" I yelled. Trigger laid back his sensitive ears. My foot came out of the stirrup as I yelled and kicked and pounded the ground. I slapped at Trigger, missed, and hit the saddle horn; it stung my hand. He jerked back with a frightened look.

"Oh, Trigger, I am so sorry." I wrapped my arms around his neck and cried. Finally, I got up and hung my smelly jacket on a fence post. I unfastened the saddle, repositioned it and pulled the cinch as tightly as possible. Finally secure on his back, I gripped the reins as Trigger pranced a few steps, settled down and cantered out of the field toward the rocky road.

Trigger's footing was especially important because he was blind.

"Ina Mae can be Trigger's eyes, and he can be her feet," Dad had said. That was the fall of 1949, the year my father decided that I needed a horse. That decision changed my life.

Once on the road, Trigger slowed to a walk when his feet felt the rocks. The road was surfaced with creek gravel, a mixture of rocks and mud, and was passable in most weather. Truck tires had dug deep ruts. Because my ankles twisted easily on uneven ground, I knew that Trigger too would need level footing, so I took him to the smoothest side of the road.

When a truck came into view, I guided Trigger to the shoulder and stopped. "Drivers may honk their horns and frighten your horse," Dad had cautioned. "Be safe; stand on the roadside until they pass. Trigger had been trained well in this practice—too well. After the truck was gone, an airplane flew overhead. At the sound of this motor, Trigger stepped to the roadside and stood motionless. I kicked my heels and flopped the reins. "Oh, come on, Trigger! That airplane won't hurt you. Let's go!" Again I yelled and pulled on the reins. In response, he reared, came down, bucked and reared again. Shaken, I decided to wait until the airplane engine noise faded. Unable to guide himself in a sightless world, Trigger could pause at the sound of an airplane if he wanted.

As we trotted the roads, cows in the fields raised their heads and horses came to the fences to exchange whinnies and watch us pass. Dogs ran behind us and barked, but slaps from the reins discouraged them. The fields were harvested, and haystacks and shocks of corn dotted the fields. My mount and I were in great spirits, and we were working together like a perfect team.

Soon the road crossed a wooden bridge over a small stream, and I slowed Trigger to a walk as we came to the wooden platform. Trigger took one step onto a plank and stopped. When I urged him forward, he shied, stepped sideways and nearly fell into the water.

"Whoa, Trigger," I pulled on the reins. "*Back*. What's wrong, boy?" We were safe on the road again. After we both were calm, I studied the bridge. Nothing was wrong. I tried to guide him back, but Trigger balked and shied. "*Hey!* What's the matter with you?" I kicked my heels into his side and tried to guide him up the middle.

He reared. I slapped his flanks as he reared and danced, again and again, until I slipped off his backside. As I hit the ground, I rolled out of range of his feet and lay there and bawled in real anger and imagined pain.

Finally I sat up, wiped my eyes on my sleeve and realized that neither of us was hurt. Trigger stood at the roadside, and I got up, walked over and petted him. I considered my plight; I could not pick roads without bridges to accommodate a frightened horse. To wait while an airplane flew over was one thing, but a mount must cross bridges. While Trigger munched some grain I gave him, I drank from my canteen and tried to think about how Dad would have handled this.

"It's your job to train the horse, and you teach him when you spot a problem," Dad had said. "You can't wait until later—not if you want him to understand." Dad would have expected me to teach Trigger to cross the bridge and to do it immediately.

After I poured water into my cupped hand and offered it to Trigger, I took the reins and led him to the center of the road. "OK, Trigger," I said softly. "Here we go." I tugged gently on the reins as I walked ahead. "One step, that's right. Now another. See? That's not so bad. Take your time. Now your hind foot. A little farther. *Good!*" The hollow sound of the boards grew less ominous as we crossed and our feet hit solid road on the other side. We crossed the bridge again, back and forth, until he no longer resisted the lead.

I took him through a ditch and into a field to position his left side next to a fence, where I mounted again and guided him back to the road. With soft words in his ears and gentle pats on his neck, Trigger walked gingerly to the edge of the bridge. I let him choose his path as he crossed to the other side. We turned around and crossed the bridge, then turned again. Leaving the bridge, we trotted all the way home. After much love and praise, my mount and I were as one again.

Was my relationship with Trigger trouble-free after that encounter? No. He had been raised and trained by a man, and he responded to a male voice faster than to mine. A man could lay a hand on his neck, speak a soft word, and that animal would do anything.

Trigger always wanted to go back the same direction we came regardless of where I wanted to go. The young people of the community played softball every Sunday afternoon at each other's homes. Unable to run, I could not play, but I kept score and cheered my friends. When we would leave for home, I would try to guide my horse in the direction I wanted to go. He would balk and try to go back the way we came. Embarrassed because I had to struggle with the horse in front of my friends, I would get angry. Invariably, one of the older boys had to come to my rescue. He could speak softly and pet Trigger's nose. Then, with reins in hand, he could lead us a few steps in the direction I wanted to go, and Trigger would trot all the way home.

But I did gain self-confidence from my experiences with the blind horse, and I learned that temper tantrums only make matters worse. A new appreciation for the limitations of man and beast has helped me see that we all must allow for each other's strengths and weaknesses.

Years have passed, and Trigger is gone. But as a teenager riding the countryside on his back, I had my first taste of independence, responsibility and the need to give as well as to take from life. My Dad's decision back then had changed my life forever.

A SPECIAL VISITOR

*A shaggy pony unexpectedly appears in
a little girl's life and stays just long enough
to capture her heart.*

BY JANE E. EVANS

"Here he comes!" I called.

I had been staring intently out the downstairs bedroom window, waiting for my father. It was a Sunday in the spring of 1942. Dad had visitation rights on Sundays, and I had been waiting eagerly for his arrival.

"He's here!" I shouted again.

Dad drove up the cinder driveway that ran alongside our large gray stone house and parked his black Chrysler in front of the three-car garage out back.

Then a second vehicle, a single-horse van, came up the driveway and stopped opposite my window. A scruffy-looking fellow with a broad-rimmed cowboy hat pulled low over his brow and a full, dense beard jumped down out of the cab. He went to the back, swung open the wide doors and pulled the ramp down onto the driveway. Then he reached inside to grab the lead shank to the animal inside and backed it slowly out of the van.

"Frampton, come here quick!" I yelled to my 5-year-old brother. "Mom, come look!" Both of them came to the window just as my father walked up to the animal—a small, brown-and-white pony with a shaggy mane and a long, equally shaggy brown-and-white tail. The pony stood quietly as Dad ran his hand down its back and along its ribs.

At the window, the three of us watched in stunned silence. For me it was like seeing a movie at the Vine Theater—lots of action but deep down, a lingering suspicion that what we were seeing wasn't really true.

"Mommy, is that pony for us?" I finally managed to ask.

"I don't know," she muttered. "Your father never said anything to me about it."

Then Frampton came alive. "Let's go see!" he shouted and raced through the house and out to the driveway. I rushed after him, my heart beating furiously. The driver handed the lead to my father. "Well, there you go," he said. "Good luck." With that he climbed into the cab, backed the van out of the driveway and drove away.

"Is he ours, Dad?"

"Yes, he's yours," he said, a broad smile on his face.

"What's his name?"

"Pete."

It was more than a 7-year-old could comprehend. I could not really imagine that Pete was ours and was going to live at our house. "Where will he stay?" I asked. "We don't have a barn."

"Well, um," Dad hesitated. "In the garage." Mother had come out to the driveway but kept a good distance away, until Dad's comment roused her. "But, Wayne...," she started.

It *was* a large garage, with three car stalls, but my mother parked her ancient Ford with the rumble seat in one stall, and another was leased to the gentleman who rented one of the five bedrooms in our house. Garden tools, baskets, toy wagons and bikes filled most of the remaining space.

"Never mind," my father said gruffly. "There's an extra stall, plenty of room." I glanced at my mother. A look of disbelief covered her face.

And so we moved Pete into the garage. We cleared an area and Dad tied Pete to one of the exposed studs. He had brought hay and feed, and there was also a water bucket that Frampton and I took turns filling. We were so eager to care for our new pet that first Sunday that Pete had a fresh bucket of water every half hour or so, whether he had taken a drink from it or not.

Later that afternoon, my father climbed back into his car and left the three of us to the care and feeding of Pete. It wasn't easy. Pete was a fairly docile pony and was good about being tied in the garage. But within a few days it became apparent that he needed more room to roam. Somewhere my mother found a long, iron pipe. With the help of a neighbor, we drove it deep into the ground in the empty lot next to our house. With a long rope extending from his halter to the stake Pete was able to wander about and munch on the grass and weeds. He spent his days outside and his nights in the garage.

This arrangement worked well for a few days, until the afternoon Pete chewed through the rope and went exploring. We didn't notice Pete was missing until the phone rang. "Your pony is in my garden," Mrs. Robinson reported. A few minutes later Mrs. Murray phoned to say Pete was in *her* garden, nibbling away at the tender young plants that were poking their heads through the soil. "Come get him now," she demanded. The moment Mother hung up, Mr. Hovey called to say Pete was munching the buds off of his backyard apple tree.

Mother rushed out to the garage, grabbed the lead and, with Frampton and me tagging along, went looking for our errant pony. We found him about three blocks away, chewing on sprouts in yet another garden. With help, we captured Pete and led him home. As Mother tied Pete to the garage stud, I again noticed the look in her face. This time it wasn't disbelief; it was anger and frustration. A chain replaced Pete's rope, so that he could no longer escape.

The more time I spent with Pete, the more I liked him. I liked giving him water and feed and even cleaning up after him in the garage. He stood passively while I brushed him, even though I did a less-than-thorough job of it.

A couple of Sundays later, Dad showed up at the garage with a saddle. "Will he let us ride him?" I asked. "He won't throw me off, will he?"

"No, of course not. He's used to somebody riding him," Dad assured me.

Struggling with the lines and straps, Dad managed to get Pete outfitted, and then he led the pony out to the driveway. Dad was right. Pete had no objection to the saddle. "My turn first," I said. Frampton stood back, looking eager but apprehensive.

With Dad holding the halter and giving me directions, I put my left foot into the stirrup, clutched the horn on the saddle and swung myself up. Never having been on a horse or pony before, it was a bit scary. I felt like I was sitting on a very tall chair. Fleetingly, I wondered if the saddle might slip around Pete's middle and leave me dangling upside down under his belly. But I soon got a firm grip on the reins and used my heels to urge Pete forward. He responded to my commands, turning slowly to the right or left as I pulled on the reins. We took a leisurely stroll up and down the driveway.

Then it was Frampton's turn. Dad held Pete's halter. "Do it just like your sister did," he instructed my brother. Frampton tried, but he couldn't raise his foot high enough to reach the stirrup. Finally, I grabbed him around the waist and gave him a boost into the saddle.

Frampton looked more like a small doll than a boy sitting up there with his skinny little legs pressed against each side of the pony's back. He held tightly to the reins, his shoes not quite reaching the stirrups. Pete was stoic; his feet were planted firmly on the ground, and he looked straight ahead. "Ready?" Dad asked my brother. Frampton didn't answer. He simply sat there, looking frozen in place.

Dad let go of the halter. Then, without so much as a twitch of his tail, Pete flattened his ears, kicked his rear legs and dumped Frampton out of the saddle and onto the driveway.

"Ow, ow!" cried Frampton as he landed on his back in the scratchy, dirty, piercing cinders. "Ow," he cried even louder, tears streaming down his face. Dad grabbed Pete's halter and led him a few feet away. I ran into the house screaming, "Mommy, Frampton's hurt!"

It took Mother a few minutes to calm Frampton down. After getting him into the house, she pulled up his shirt. Driveway cinders were embedded into the skin near the center of Frampton's spine. Carefully, and with Frampton whimpering for good reason, she used tweezers to remove as many of the little black, burnt pieces as she could. Some were too deep to be taken out. Over the next few weeks, the skin healed over them, and they would remain in my brother's back for the rest of his life.

The school year was coming to an end. The last day of school in early June was a week away; Pete had been with us for a little over a month. On Monday morning of that last week of school my teacher, Miss Rose, announced that there would be a special surprise right after lunch.

"What do you suppose it is?" my classmates asked one another.

"Maybe ice cream."

"Maybe we get to go home early."

"Maybe we'll have gym today instead of tomorrow."

I had no idea, except that treats always meant some time away from workbook assignments such as the dreaded math word problems. The morning droned on, and lunchtime came and went. "All right, class," Miss Rose said. "Get on your hats and coats. It's a bit chilly outside. We're going out to the playground."

All 27 of us trooped out to the grassy far end of the playground, and there, waiting for us, was my mother, standing beside Pete the pony. I was astonished. Mother had never hinted that she was bringing him to school. She held Pete by the lead; he was all dressed in his halter, reins, saddle and stirrups.

My classmates had lots of questions: "Where do you keep him?" "What does he eat?" "Does he bite?" My mother patiently answered each one. "Can we ride him?" someone called out.

"No, but this is Jane's pony," she said. "She will show you how she can ride Pete." Many "oohs" and "aahs" came from my classmates. For the second time that afternoon, I was astonished. I was going to ride Pete in front of the whole class—and what seemed to me, the whole world.

With as much grace as I could muster, I walked to Pete's side, put my foot into the stirrup and pulled myself into the saddle. What a wonderful feeling to be high above the other children. Skillfully, I pulled the reins and walked Pete away from the group. Then, an inspiration: I would gallop Pete around the grassy area! Digging my heels into Pete's side I shouted "giddy-up!" Pete responded wonderfully; he took off at a full run as I leaned down over his neck.

"Good boy, Pete," I called. I was being jiggled around in the saddle and took a tighter grip on the reins. We raced around the playground twice before I reined him to a halt. The two of us— Pete and I—were breathing heavily. Since I had started riding him, we had never gone any faster than a slow walk. I slid out of the saddle to the ground. My knees felt like they might collapse, but they held. My classmates were clapping and shouting "hurrah!" as I walked back, feelings of pride and confidence swelling in my chest. I was a momentary heroine, and Pete had made it all possible.

But that was the one and only appearance of Jane and Pete. On the last day of school I went out into our yard and saw that Pete was not tied in the empty lot. I checked the garage. He was not there, either.

"Where's Pete?" I asked Mother as I came running through the back door into the kitchen.

"He's gone to a new home," she replied.

"But, why?"

"Your father will explain it to you," was all she had to say. Dad never had much to say about Pete, except that he had found a good place for him. It was clear that I was not to ask any more questions.

That summer was filled with the usual activities—swimming down at the dam, pickup baseball games in a vacant lot, an outing at the Burton Fair where we watched harness racing. But I missed Pete greatly and thought of him often.

In the middle of a hot, humid night I awoke from a fitful sleep and started thinking about Pete again. Where did he go? Did he really have a good home? Would I ever see him again? Little tears squeezed out of the corners of my eyes. Sadness and disappointment filled my heart and head. Why hadn't my parents seen how much Pete meant to me? Why did they take him away?

One fall afternoon as I was walking home from a friend's house, I saw a single horse trailer pulled by a pickup truck traveling down our street. As it passed I could see the rump of the animal inside. It was brown and white. My heart quickened, and I started running after the trailer calling "Pete, Pete." I stopped, realizing I couldn't possibly catch it. Then, just as the trailer disappeared out of my sight I heard a loud, long, high-pitched whinny. "Pete, Pete," I yelled again. There was no answer. "That was him," I said to myself. "I know it was Pete. He was calling to me."

I took the shortcut home, through the vacant field next to our house. Near the path was the iron stake that had kept Pete from wandering away. It was rusted and almost hidden under the fallen leaves and dead grass. I stopped when I saw it, and that same sad feeling and all those haunting questions came back to me. After a moment I turned away and, shuffling my shoes through the dry dirt, headed home. Turning around, I took one last look at the iron stake. It had become for me a silent memorial to Pete, the pony I had loved and lost.

TIES THAT BIND

On a special night at the Meadowlands, a filly
orphaned shortly after birth and the man who helped
her survive are reunited in the winner's circle.

By William P. Hayden

As manager of Doc's Farm, a large Standardbred breeding operation in Far Hills, New Jersey, I am always on the go with all there
is to be done, especially in the spring. Nonetheless I still distinctly remember a beautiful, sunny June day back in 1997. It was the
kind of late spring day when everything around you is busy,
bursting with new life and clothed in that special shade of green
made almost translucent by the sun. On that beautiful day I
received an unexpected phone call from Brendan Furlong, MVB,
who was at his veterinary clinic in Oldwick, New Jersey. I was definitely not prepared for the outcome of the call, nor did I know
that it would change my life forever.

Dr. Furlong explained that a 19-year-old Standardbred mare,
Miss Falcon, had died after giving birth to a feisty little filly.
Fortunately, the mare had lived long enough to give her baby the
colostrum needed for survival. Doc Furlong and his staff had
been taking turns bottle-feeding the little filly, and thanks to their
excellent care, she was going strong. However, Doc Furlong said,
the owners of the mare did not want to incur any more expenses,

so there was some talk back and forth between them about putting the foal to sleep. When I heard that, I immediately hooked up our horse trailer and headed off to the clinic.

When I arrived and stepped into the filly's stall for the first time, it was, well, love at first sight. This little handful of fluff stared at me as if to say, "You let them put me to sleep and YOU will lose a lot of sleep." That was it: I was in—hook, line and sinker. So I lifted this little fluffball into my arms and placed her gently in the bed of straw I had prepared for her in the trailer. I had brought along Tom, my assistant manager, to ride in the trailer with the filly to keep her calm.

Before we left, I paid the veterinary bill, which was a grand total of $500, and was given the filly's papers. I had myself an orphan! Being an orphan myself, I figured we had a lot in common. In fact, as I drove carefully back to Doc's Farm, it struck me then that my new little filly's name should be Lil Orphan Annie.

The responsibility I had taken upon myself was challenging to the point of sometimes being overwhelming. Bottle-feeding a young foal is exacting and time-consuming. Annie needed to be fed four times through the day and then again four times during the night. However, some of our farm tenants welcomed Annie into their hearts, too, and took turns making the formula and bottle-feeding her. I handled the middle-of-the-night feedings and, when the alarm clock woke me night after night, you can bet I truly appreciated the expression "a sleep-deprived new mother."

As exhausted as we all were, we somehow made it through those early days, fussing over Annie like mother hens, clucking and cooing. Annie, in return, blossomed with the season. What a joy it was to see her wobbly little legs grow and strengthen and her ribs fill out. She sprinted and bucked and poked her nose practically everywhere those first three months!

Soon it was time to wean Annie and get her on some solid

feed. I realized it was time to wean her from people, too, because it was obvious to all that she was a spoiled brat. It was difficult trying to walk that fine line between giving this little orphan the closeness she needed early on and encouraging her to develop the independence she needed now. Naturally, she followed me wherever I went, and I discovered weaning was going to be a little painful for me, too. It was weaning time on Doc's Farm as well, so I picked the most docile filly we had and put her with Annie. With the other filly missing her mom and Annie missing me, the two finally bonded.

As the months passed, Annie settled in with the whole group of youngsters, but her personality really stood out. She didn't take any guff from anyone! But one of the most heartwarming things about her was how she would always come when I called to her, even from way across the pasture when she was with the others. She would always come for a nuzzle, a good rough hug and, most of all—her favorite—having her neck scratched. Then, I'd go back to my work, and Annie would stroll off to rejoin the other fillies. We had done it: Annie was independent and no longer in danger of being spoiled rotten by people, but she and I were still able to share a very special bond.

My next step was to register Annie with the United States Trotting Association (USTA). I was afraid the name "Lil Orphan Annie" had already been used and that I would have to choose another. But to my surprise, the name was available, so Annie kept her name.

When she finally became a yearling, it was time for me to make some important decisions. While I would have loved to have sent her to a trainer at the racetrack, I had to face the fact that this would not be possible on a farm manager's salary. I did give some thought to a partnership, but some prior experiences had soured me on this approach.

I had to face it: The only option I had was to put Annie in a good yearling sale. My goal was to get Annie into the best sale that I could. Her breeding was not too bad—she was by a stallion named Laag, who had earned well over a million dollars—but her sisters and brothers had not done well at the tracks. I sent an application to a prestigious sale in Kentucky, but Annie wasn't accepted. She wasn't considered good enough for the second sale I tried, either, so the only option left to me was to put her in our local New Jersey sale. Though it is not a very prestigious sale, I was happy that Annie could be sold to someone nearby. It was going to be hard to give her up, and at least this way I could keep an eye on her.

I never gave much thought to the amount of money Annie would bring, but I did feel it was only fair that she have a chance to prove herself at the racetrack. I shipped Annie to a good friend's farm, Boxwood Farm, in Englishtown, New Jersey. Boxwood Farm specializes in getting horses to look good for sales. Taylor Palmer, the owner, generously waived the prepping fee; I just had to pay for board.

It was very sad here at Doc's Farm the day Annie left. There was no shortage of tears. It just seemed impossible that she would no longer be poking her nose around, shoving us playfully, and making us laugh with her antics in the fields with the other fillies. The day of the sale, I was a nervous wreck. Knowing the horse business pretty much inside and out, I had decided that if it looked like Annie was heading for a stable or owner that I didn't approve of, I would buy her back. Well, Annie brought $3,000 at the sale, a paltry sum compared to the bids of $100,000 and more that were made on some of the other yearlings. But I was pleased with her new owners, and I knew Annie would be treated well.

Although it was hard, as time passed, I finally managed to get Annie out of my mind by concentrating on some of the other horses at the farm. Then, around a year after she was sold, I turned to the local newspaper's racing section—something I do every day, mostly looking to see if any Doc's Farm horses might be racing that night. I heard myself gasp when I saw Annie's name. "Lil Orphan Annie," in bold print on the entries list, practically jumped off the page at me. She was going to compete in the June 17, 1999, New Jersey Sire Stakes for 2-year-old fillies for a purse of $30,000! On top of that, the race was at the Meadowlands, a premier harness track that is only an hour's drive from our farm.

I felt delirious. I wandered around telling anyone who would listen, "My God! She has never been in a race, and they put her in a $30,000 stakes race." To make matters worse, Annie had drawn the number 8 post, an outside position that would pose a challenge even for an experienced racehorse.

Well, I can tell you, I got my chores done early that day, fed all of the horses earlier than usual, put on my Sunday best for Annie and headed to the track with a heart full of emotions, some of them conflicting. I felt concerned for Annie in a race that big, never having raced before, and most of all, I didn't want her to get injured. I was also incredibly happy and proud. I would see her again! And she must be in great condition to have been entered at all. "OK, OK," I told myself, "calm down. If Annie just *finishes* the race, it will be a victory for a raw novice like her."

At the track, to no one's surprise, Annie was listed at 25 to 1, the longest shot of the race. As I recall, the comment by the handicapper in the race program was, "This is asking a lot of this youngster." Down deep, I was inclined to agree with him. Just for fun, I placed bets of $2 to win, $2 to place and $2 to show on Annie. How could I not give her at least that small vote of confidence?

My heart was pounding as the race began. Annie got off to a

pretty good start, but never went to the lead. She hung around fifth most of the race and then started to back off. At this point, I was telling my friends how happy I was that she at least made it to the big track. Then it happened! Over the loudspeaker, I heard her name, "And it's Lil Orphan Annie, who seems to have found another gear, and she is charging on the outside, and she's fourth, and third. Ladies and Gentlemen, I see an upset brewing here— yes, folks, it's Lil Orphan Annie winning her first race ever in 1:56 3/5—a new lifetime mark—at better than 29 to 1!"

I cannot begin to describe how I felt. Now I really was delirious! There was quite a delay taking the winner's circle picture, as I had to be literally dragged back from hugging Annie and planting a big, sloppy kiss on her forehead. She knew. I knew she knew. And in those few brief moments, I felt as if she was saying to me, "This one's for you, Willie, for saving my life." The new owner was so happy, he was crying, too, and just before he left the winner's circle, I reached into my wallet and gave him what I had been carrying around with me for over a year: a picture of Annie nursing from a bottle that I was holding.

I sure do miss Annie, but I can't help but think that maybe— just maybe—and God willing, we'll be together again someday.

TRAVELING WITH
THE AMBASSADOR

*Have horse, will travel. That's this volunteer's
motto when she takes her American
Miniature Horse on the road.*

BY DENISE J. PULLIS

Last February, an ambassador visited my son's elementary
school. As she stepped from the back seat of a Jeep Cherokee, 60
children lined up to meet her, squirming with excitement. The
ambassador looked them over, sniffed their pockets and offered
to shake hands.

This ambassador did not come from a country with unusual customs. Her diplomatic visits will not bring peace to a troubled
world. But her whiskery kisses bring laughter and love wherever
she goes. She is Mercy Bo Cool, an American Miniature Horse.

Standing 32 inches tall at the withers (American
Miniatures are measured in inches rather than hands), Mercy
may be small, but she is still a horse in every sense of the word.
She trots, canters, gallops and jumps (nailing those lead changes
with no rider aboard), pulls a cart and can negotiate an obstacle
course. What baffles the average horseperson who sees her is why
anyone would prefer a pocket equine when he or she could be
enjoying a ride on a "normal" horse.

For me, horses are more than mere "recreational vehicles" that go when you put a heel or a stick to them—they are companion animals, too. They like to have a herd to identify with, and Mercy definitely identifies with my family "herd." In the course of her travels, Mercy helps both horse lovers and people who aren't familiar with horses to share the vision that these four-legged friends are not just for riding.

Mercy's career began with an invitation to participate in an open house at our local volunteer ambulance corps. A neighbor, intrigued by my description and photos of the little horse, had thought that kids at the open house would enjoy her. "Could you bring her?" he asked hopefully.

"Yes," I blurted out, simultaneously wondering how I would get her there without a trailer. My husband, Tim, read my mind and said, "Rent one. Somebody should have one just sitting around."

A discouraging search began. People I knew who had trailers were shipping their own horses that weekend or wanted a large sum of money for their services or were just not interested. My last hope was a phone call to a friend of a friend. She, too, was busy, but she offered a unique solution: "Why not take her in the car?"

Strange as it may seem to large-horse enthusiasts, American Miniatures have a distinct advantage over large horses when it comes to shipping: They can, and do, fit in sport utility vehicles and minivans. Although I had transported Mercy this way as a weanling, I had not thought of it for an adult miniature.

"I did when she was a baby, but now she weighs 200 pounds and wouldn't fit in the cargo area of my Cherokee," I said. "Tell me more!"

"I worked for a miniature-horse farm, and they would ship the horses in their Blazer," the woman told me. "They took the seat out of the back, and the horses jumped in. You could try that option." She outlined a training regimen that would have a cooperative Mercy traveling by car within a week.

Eager to begin, my sons, Andrew and Benjamin, and I prepared the Cherokee for its newest occupant. We removed the back seat entirely, padded and tarped the floor, and opened the doors. Mercy watched from a nearby paddock. To her, the Cherokee was an enormous lunch box from which her human family got treats for her. She nickered approvingly.

First, I placed a bale of shavings for a step near the car door where Mercy would enter. Next, I applied a set of tiny shipping boots to Mercy's dainty legs. After lifting her feet high for a minute or two, Mercy was accustomed to the boots, and she followed me to the car. I fished a carrot out of my pocket and dangled it in front of her nose as I climbed into the car. Mercy placed her front hooves on the bale of shavings and stretched out her neck, head and nose, lipping the air to reach the treat that was just beyond her reach. Then she stepped down, swishing her tail in frustration.

"Why won't she go in?" asked Andrew. "She loves carrots." "Try again," Benjamin said, patting the filly and whispering in her ear. "I know you can do it, Mercy."

Again Mercy placed her little hooves on the bale and craned her neck into the Cherokee, sniffing everything her nose could touch. The carrot was just out of reach, tempting her, but she did not make the final jump into the car. Once again, she backed down, swishing her tail like a lash and rolling her eyes in confusion. Her body language clearly said, "What do you people want from me? I don't understand. I can't fit in there. You're teasing me with that carrot, and I have had enough of this!"

"What is she saying?" asked Andrew. I thought hard.

"Benjamin, please get me a can of grain. Andrew, next

time she gets her feet on the bale, let's have you push her butt toward the door so that her body is straight. I think she is afraid she is going to bang herself on that door frame if she tries to jump in." As the boys assisted me, I warned them, "She may jump in this time. If she does, do *not* jump in behind her, in case she gets scared or kicks!" The boys nodded.

Andrew placed his hands on Mercy's rump as she climbed onto the bale. I shook the can of grain, and the mare's ears went forward. As Mercy poked her nose into the car, Andrew gently pushed her body straight, and her expression brightened. It was as if the proverbial light bulb had gone on in her head. "Oh, now I get it! You want me to jump in *here!*"

With a mighty heave, she sailed into the car and received her reward. Before I could stop them, the boys had pushed Mercy's rump aside and climbed in next to her. Mercy was too interested in her new surroundings and tasty treat to mind the intrusion.

"She did it!" Andrew and Benjamin cheered. "Now what?"

"She gets out, and we try again. And this time, don't climb in behind her. She could kick," I said unconvincingly.

I crawled out, followed by Mercy. Then I turned around and invited the little horse to enter the Cherokee again. Without hesitation, she jumped in. This was a fun game. Jump in—get a pat and a treat. Jump out—get a pat. It was definitely better to jump in!

For two days, we practiced this routine. It got to the point that when Mercy saw her red and black shipping boots, she would nicker and nod her head in anticipation. Over the next two days, she adjusted with growing aplomb to the closing of the door, the starting of the engine and the squealing of the two boys.

Finally, it was time to let her feel the car in motion. The routine was the same: Catch Mercy, groom her, put on the shipping boots, get her in the car, get Andrew and Benjamin in the car, close the doors, start the engine. But now..."Here we go!" I said. The boys held Mercy's head and patted her. She looked out her window, enjoying the view. I backed the Cherokee up, taking care to move slowly so Mercy could keep her balance.

"She can do it!" the boys exclaimed. "Go, Mercy!"

We drove up and down the driveway several times before I was convinced that this would actually work. Mercy behaved as she always has: curious yet quiet, and very willing to do what's asked when she understands what it is. When I stopped the car, she waited patiently for me to open her door before she jumped out and gave a great shake like a wet dog.

My husband was not as thrilled with Mercy's accomplishments as the boys and I were, however. "You're crazy!" Tim said. "Are you going to ride with that horse in your car?"

"I have no other option. She is well-behaved and seems to like it." He shook his head in silent disapproval.

The open house was on a sunny October day. Tim waited to follow me with the boys in his car while I loaded Mercy and started off. The first part of the trip was quiet, as we passed through areas with few houses. But as we approached the town and traffic became heavier, I started getting those looks I remembered from Mercy's very first car ride—people wondering if the coffee at breakfast might have been spiked, if their eyeglasses were dirty, if that was some kind of fuzzy dog in the silver Cherokee ahead of them. Then came the final look of astonishment, accompanied by pointing fingers, as they realized they were seeing a horse in a car. Unconcerned, Mercy stared back at them and chewed a mouthful of hay.

At the ambulance corps building, I parked the car. Mercy anxiously pawed at the door as Tim pulled in next to us and got out with a smile. He, too, had seen the funny looks and pointing.

"It comes with the territory," I told him nonchalantly.

My neighbor rushed out to greet us, followed by the children and adults who had gathered to see "the little horse that rides in a car." Mercy quickly settled into her role as ambassador for miniature horses, patiently enduring the fuss as people patted her, hugged her and offered her handfuls of hay. She even tolerated a visiting medical helicopter that landed nearby, as well as the sirens of the ambulances, without lifting her head from her hay pile.

The best part of the day was the response from the children. It made the three hours of volunteer work very rewarding—even more fun than my best rides on those large horses. It began with the question kids always ask first: "Can we ride her?" My answer is always, "No, she is too little." As they venture closer to find out what redeeming values this little horse has (if you can't ride her, what is she good for?), their eyes open with new discoveries about horses.

"She is so soft! I did not know horses were so soft."

"She smells so clean." (A bath and coat conditioner helped here.)

"I never touched a horse before. I like the way she feels."

"Wow! She can shake hands and give kisses like my dog."

"She's nice! Is she for sale? Can I take her home?" It was good to see people view horses in a new way. Children who might have been timid around a larger horse became brave in Mercy's presence—first, touching her, then hugging her, and finally, shaking "hands" with her. Even the parents, who initially stood back, began to edge closer, reaching out to a different horse experience.

Little by little, the word has spread about my miniature ambassador. These days, Mercy receives invitations to visit schools, fund-raisers and other activities, where she and I continue to educate children and adults on what horses are really like "in person." Having solved my trailer problem for the moment, I can take her anywhere without having to worry about parking a truck-and-trailer combination. On my tight budget, the Cherokee has been a welcome method of horse transportation (for short distances). Still, out of my three American Miniatures, only Mercy has the temperament to use it safely. It has been fun to travel with Mercy, watching her look out the windows as she wonders where she is going, who she will meet and—most important—what kinds of treats they will have for her.

Author's note: Although my sons rode in the cargo area of the Cherokee during Mercy's training, that was on our farm property and not on open roads. During official trips, the boys ride with my husband or event organizers, in vehicles where they can use safety belts.

A PONY FOR RAHZARO

*Finding a companion for their lonely horse was
harder than they expected. Then winter blew
a solution right to their barn door.*

BY KRISTIN NELSON

Something had to be done about Rahzaro. Living alone was not
just making my aged horse neurotic; it was starting to threaten
his health. For the second year since we'd moved to our country
place, a small farm chosen because it had a barn for Rahzaro, he
was heading into winter resolutely rooted to the spot where our
pasture fence intersected with the neighbor's. He refused to stay
in his barn. No sooner had he eaten his rations each day than
he'd be off to his post again. It was the one corner of the property where he could keep an eye on the neighbor's horses.

We tried to humor the 24-year-old gelding: We left the barn
door open, allowing him to come and go at will; we hauled hay
up to him at the fence; we scheduled his yearly veterinary checkup for a sunny day so it could be performed outside. This
approach didn't sit well with the farrier, however, who couldn't
be expected to lug anvil and forge up the hill to Rahzaro's corner.
He pronounced the gelding "barn sour," and it was true. But it
wasn't our barn Rahzaro longed for. It was the neighbor's barn—
and the neighbor's horses, tantalizingly visible in the distance.

My husband and I decided Rahzaro needed a friend. We would get him a pony, we thought—an older one that no one wanted anymore. That seemed simple enough. From talking to the neighbors, the farrier and our veterinarian, I gleaned a consensus that I should be able to find an outgrown children's pony for about $50.

I started checking newspaper ads and feed-store bulletin boards. There were a few ponies listed, but they tended to fall into the "show home preferred/$1,000 firm" category. I called the Humane Society to see if I could rescue a pony, but they dealt only with dogs and cats. I considered attending the monthly livestock auction in a small town south of us, but we didn't have a trailer, and I couldn't stand to face all the animals I would feel sorry for. I even thought of placing a "Pony Wanted" ad, but it seemed a little presumptuous to ask people to practically give you their pony. Little did I know that all this time the answer to our problem was standing in a pasture less than a mile from our house—but hell would have to practically freeze over before we found him.

The climate in our part of Washington state is usually bearable in the cold months, but the winter of 1989 proved the exception. In January, a record high-pressure ridge anchored itself over Alaska and Canada and sent our temperatures into single digits. Even Bob's relatives in Minnesota were sympathetic. One week, the filters on our well froze, leaving us without water until they thawed. Rahzaro's only concession to the weather was to move a few feet to his right, putting the well house between himself and the wind. I put a fleece-lined blanket on him and despaired of digging the ice out of his feet with anything so puny as a hoof pick. I hated to leave him every day to go to work, but it was one morning when we were heading out to our jobs that his luck finally changed.

Stopped on the shoulder of the road in front of our house was a young girl leading two bareback horses. The wind was whipping the snow around the horses' legs and lifting their manes. Having evidently decided to ride one horse and lead the other, the girl was trying to climb up on the larger of the two. But the horses were skittish, and she was having no luck. We got out of the car. Bob reached the girl first, and she told him she was on her way home with her mare, who was in foal. Because her family didn't have a barn yet on their farm, she said, they had been concerned about the mare in the extreme weather. So they had left her with some friends who had a barn near us. But their stalls weren't screened, and the other horses had picked on her.

"We have just the deal for you," we said. Not only were the stalls in our barn screened, we told the girl, but even if they weren't, the only other possible occupant stayed inside just long enough to eat his grain and some of his hay. She accepted our offer gratefully. In quick succession, we got the mare (named Spice) settled in a stall, made sure the young girl (named Danielle) could reach us in case of disaster, and left for work.

It was well after dark when we returned. As usual, my first order of business was to check on Rahzaro. He had ignored us that morning, since nothing that went on in the barn could possibly interest him. I didn't see him in his fence corner, set off by the moonlight, and I didn't see him right away when I went in the barn. Curious, I peered around the door of his stall, and there he was. For the first time since we'd owned the place, he was in the barn at night, napping on the floor of his stall. His feet were curled up under him, and the ice packed in his shoes had completely melted away.

Rahzaro spent the whole night in the barn. I saw him in the morning from the kitchen window, sauntering out to brag to the neighbor horses that he had a cute visitor over at his place.

Spice stayed with us for almost a week, until the weather eased, and although Rahzaro still insisted on being outside during the day, he spent each night safe and warm in his stall.

Every day, Danielle and her mother, Colleen, came over to feed the mare and take her out for some exercise. They were grateful for the use of the stall and asked several times what they could do for us in return. Actually, they were doing *us* a favor, I told them. I told them of our ongoing problem with Rahzaro, and described how we had tried to get him a friend but had been unable to find one. Spice had come along just in time, I said. In fact, I added, Rahzaro adored the mare so much that they couldn't take her home unless they replaced her.

I was just kidding, but a look passed between mother and daughter. Well, they said, there is always Bear.

Bear, it turned out, was the senior member of their herd and Danielle's first pony. He was about 20 years old, and she had outgrown him. They hadn't actually considered selling him, but they would talk to the rest of the family and see what they thought. It was my turn to exchange looks with Bob. An outgrown children's pony right down the street, and now almost in our grasp. Fate wasn't usually this kind.

On the night Spice went home, Rahzaro resumed his post at the fence and wouldn't come in the barn. If things didn't work out with the pony, Bob and I didn't know what we'd do. But the next morning, Colleen called us with good news. Not only was Bear available; they had decided to give him to us for free. They asked only that we promise to take good care of him and never sell him.

Yes, of course, we told her, but we insisted that she let us pay for him. Colleen wouldn't hear of it. They had paid just $50 for Bear themselves three years before (I guess that was the going rate, after all), and that price had included a saddle.

Rahzaro didn't know what was coming, or he would have been as excited as I was the next weekend when we walked down the street to bring Bear home. Still, the old gelding perked up quickly when we put Bear in the paddock next to him. In fact, he couldn't take his eyes off the round and fuzzy pony. Unconcerned, Bear poked around his new home, investigating the grazing options and totally ignoring his new neighbor.

Although Colleen had told me that Bear got along with anyone, I kept the two separate for the first day. But by that evening, the chestnut gelding and the black-and-white pony were dozing side by side, with only the fence between them. It was obvious my horse's life had taken a permanent turn for the better.

So began eight years of genial companionship. Rahzaro and Bear remained friends for the rest of their lives. They were a study in contrasts—not just in size but in personality. Rahzaro, the seven-eighths Arabian, was a gregarious people-pleaser who even liked the veterinarian, and Bear, the Shetland cross, was an independent loner who knew the value of a well-aimed kick. Now that they are gone, the one thing that's most important to me about these two old friends is how much I miss them both.

CHAPTER 4

THANKS FOR THE MEMORIES

THANK YOU, BLAZE

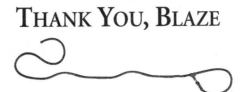

*The sturdy chestnut gelding had always
trusted his owners to do the right thing.
This time, his life was on the line.*

BY MARK A. COSGROVE

Blaze was sick. My mind raced as I drove to the veterinary teaching hospital at Michigan State University with the chestnut gelding in the trailer behind me. I kept going over the events that had led up to this trip. I was worried.

The stocky Quarter Horse with one white sock and, of course, a white blaze on his face had been in our family for several years. Always a bit on the heavy side, he was the very definition of an "easy keeper." He came to us as the victim of the maturing process—not his own, but his previous owner's. The teenage girl who had once lived and breathed horses was now grown up, married and a mother, with little time left to devote to her horse. She realized that he needed a new home, with a young girl to care for and love him as she had done. We were fortunate to be that home. We purchased Blaze for our daughter, Allison, who was a beginning rider and a member of the local 4-H riding club.

When Blaze arrived, he hadn't been ridden regularly for some time. He was out of shape and somewhat rusty. But before long, it was evident that he had been trained well and knew far more than we did. He excelled at Western events and was competitive in English classes. By the time Allison and Blaze began their first 4-H season together, there was already a close bond between them, and as Allison continued to learn, Blaze took care of her. He knew what was expected, and even when given the wrong cues he tried to do what he knew was right.

I remember one incident during their second season together, when Allison was executing a basic reining pattern. She gave the cues for a rollback on the wrong side. Blaze resisted and tried to go the other way. Allison fought him and insisted he turn in the opposite direction. He finally obeyed. As she rode up for her tack check at the end of the pattern, the judge told her she had done well, but her rollbacks were in the wrong direction. You could almost see Blaze thinking, "I *tried* to tell you."

As good as Blaze's training was, it was not his most valuable asset. He was kind. He liked people. Whenever he saw someone approaching the paddock, he would nicker and come to the fence. You didn't need to bring him food—just some attention was fine. And he was trustworthy. He knew the difference between an experienced rider and a novice. If I placed a small child on his back, he knew to be careful. I would tell him to come along, and he would follow me slowly around the arena at my shoulder, without a lead. The child would hold the reins, thinking, "I'm doing this all by myself." Only Blaze and I knew better.

Allison and Blaze did well as a team over the years. They achieved the county show's "High Point Award" for Western pleasure one season, and qualified for the state show twice. Eventually, we decided it was time for Allison to take on a greater challenge. We purchased a younger, more athletic horse for her and started Blaze on his third career—helping Andrew, our nine-year-old, learn how to ride.

As a beginner, Andrew entered walk-trot classes. He was so proud when he received his first ribbon. The next season, he and

Blaze did quite well, gaining confidence and even cantering. They were becoming a team. But things did not always go smoothly. Once, while getting ready for a show, Andrew tied Blaze to a hitch, leaving too much slack in the rope. The gelding started to graze and got his lead wrapped around his lower leg. As the rope tightened, he pulled away. It was at that instant that I spotted him, lead rope tight, fear in his eyes, holding his leg suspended in the air.

"Blaze, whoa!" I yelled.

Blaze froze and looked at me, his leg still in the air. I rushed toward him from about 20 feet away, sure that he would panic and injure himself before I could get there. He did not. He just stood still, waiting—trusting that I would help him. I yanked hard on the quick-release knot, and he was free. The leg was hurt, but only slightly. Icing solved the problem, and two days later he was fine. Andrew learned a valuable lesson about securing his horse, and Blaze again demonstrated what a remarkable animal he was, defying his instincts and relying on me to get him out of the jam.

Last fall, as the show season ended, Blaze looked the best he ever had. He was well muscled and trim, having shed those few extra pounds he always seemed to carry. It was time for a break. We pulled his shoes and let him settle in for the winter, increasing his time on pasture. But instead of putting on weight, he continued to lose.

I suspected worms, even though Blaze was on a deworming program. I dewormed him again. No change. Soon his weight loss became apparent, with ribs starting to show. One evening, when I opened the gate to turn the horses out to pasture, Blaze didn't take off for his evening meal. He just stood there, looking for a few minutes at the open gate; then he slowly turned and walked back toward his lean-to. I called the veterinarian.

At first, Blaze was treated for Potomac horse fever. A case had just occurred on a neighboring farm, and some clinical signs indicated that as a possibility. When the blood tests returned, however, the results were negative. By now, the sadly diminished gelding was hardly eating at all. I tried everything I could think of, or that somebody else suggested—different feeds, bran mash, apples, carrots, molasses, anything I thought might get him to eat. He would not. I called the university for an appointment.

Still trying to make sense of it all, I pulled into the Michigan State Veterinary Teaching Hospital parking lot. I was told where to unload and instructed to take my horse to a holding stall. Blaze walked next to me, ever so slowly, weak and unsteady. Two veterinary students appeared. They took his history and performed a preliminary exam. Soon the veterinarian arrived and instructed the students to weigh Blaze and move him to the "quiet room" for further examination. He weighed in at 916 pounds, almost 200 pounds below normal.

In the examining room, the doctor guided the students as they completed their workup, and then he examined Blaze himself. There was much discussion about possible causes, and the results of the blood tests were discussed extensively. Few clues seemed to be emerging to explain the weight loss until the doctor listened to Blaze's lungs. Noting some differences in breathing sounds, he proceeded to do an ultrasound. On the screen, he pointed out to me a large quantity of fluid in the chest cavity. Next, he found another collection of fluid in the abdominal cavity.

It was at this point that the veterinarian stopped the examination and spoke with me about what he had found. There were several things that could cause the large buildup of fluid, he told me, but none of them offered a good prognosis. His first thought was cancer. As he spoke, I felt my face flush and my eyes start to water. Standing next to Blaze, this horse who had meant so much to our family, I heard my worst fears realized.

The veterinarian said he would like to take samples of the horse's chest and abdominal fluids to have them analyzed. This could confirm his diagnosis. I told him to go ahead. Then he took me aside and spoke to me in a lower voice. It was his opinion, he said, that Blaze would continue to worsen over the next two to three weeks. He paused, drew a breath and told me that soon we would have to make a decision to put the horse to sleep. I nodded. I couldn't speak. It hit me then, the full impact of what this kind and gentle horse meant to me. Blaze would try to do anything that was asked of him. I had trusted my children with him. He had never let me down.

I stood by and patted Blaze as they drew fluid from his abdomen and chest. The veterinarian told me I could take him home, and he would call with the test results that evening.

I couldn't do it. I couldn't take our horse home, tell my family what the prognosis was and then bring him back to be destroyed. I told this to the doctor, and he understood. He said he would hospitalize Blaze, pending the results of the tests. As I was checking out, he asked me if I wanted to sign an authorization to have Blaze euthanatized. That would only occur, he said, after my verbal authorization, once the results were in and the diagnosis was confirmed. I signed quickly, and the doctor assured me he would call that evening.

I went back to the holding stall. I had a carrot in my pocket. I pulled it out and tried to get Blaze to take it. He would not. I petted him and spoke to him. I told him I was sorry. Then I opened the stall door, walked out and closed it behind me.

I started to walk away, but I couldn't leave. I came back, entered the stall and hugged Blaze. He stood quietly as I told him good-bye.

That evening we waited for the phone call. Around 9 p.m., it came.

"I think we have some answers," the doctor began. "There are cancer cells in the chest fluid. I'm very sorry."

"I see," I responded, trying to control my emotions.

There was a short silence. The doctor asked, "Do you want us to go ahead and...?"

"Yes," I interrupted.

"We share your sorrow," he said. "You're doing the right thing."

I thanked him for his help and sensitivity and hung up the phone. There was no need to explain what my wife and children had just heard. The tears flowed freely. As I tried to console my son and daughter, I spoke to them about being thankful for what Blaze had given us. This large animal, so strong and powerful, I said, had been our gentle friend and, in reality, part of our family.

Blaze is gone now, but he has left us with memories. More than that, he has left us with knowledge. Not only did he help my daughter and my son and me to understand the many facets of caring for and riding horses; he also taught us about the closeness, respect and love that occurs when people and animals work together as a team. We have had several horses, but the special relationship we had with Blaze is something we will cherish for the rest of our lives.

When I think of him now, I whisper out loud to him, hoping that he will hear, "Thank you, Blaze."

FOREVER YOUNG

When Timbrooks arrived, he was already 20.
But the spunky Tennessee Walking Horse was
nowhere near ready for retirement.

BY LINDA SPRAGUE

It started on shaky ground, this partnership of an aged Tennessee Walking Horse and a woman who hadn't a clue what Walkers were about. But it would last for two decades and bring joy to all who knew my gentle, generous Timmy.

I grew up on Long Island in the 1950s and started my riding career at 10, thanks to a childhood buddy. Gini had her own horse. (To me, that was akin to having your own rocket ship.) She showed me how to groom and tack, and I accompanied her and her family to the many gymkhanas held on the island back then. Eventually, as young girls do, we drifted apart. Gini went to a different school, and I lost touch with her.

It would be 10 years before I got my own horse. No more Western saddles for me: I was about to enter the hunter-jumper scene. All those shows at Melody Farms and C.W. Post were so exciting. We won some ribbons, though I knew I didn't have what it takes to continue. Still, I kept my horse. With a full-time job and a husband, my riding was strictly for pleasure.

In 1977, our neighbor purchased an aged Tennessee

Walking Horse gelding, a large blue roan named Timbrooks. I would see the two of them shuffling along from time to time and wonder what the ride felt like, but I was much too traditional in my tastes to find out. Timmy turned out to be a handful for his rider, however, and she quickly lost interest in him. He languished for a year. I could see he was depressed, and he began weaving.

Hating to see any horse unhappy, I inquired whether my husband, Butch, could ride Timmy. His owner agreed, delighted to have someone show an interest in the aged gelding. Though Butch is not a serious rider, he has a good seat and quiet hands, and he and Timmy soon became a pair. Our neighbor, realizing that no one was going to buy a 20-year-old horse, offered him to us. "Just give him a good home," she said—and we did.

Since Butch is a car enthusiast, he soon decided that driving a carriage—even at only one horsepower—would be more fun than riding. I was dubious. Butch knew nothing about harness and carriages, and, for all we knew, neither did Timmy. But in two weeks' time, they were driving confidently through the wonderful trails of Connetquot Park. Aunts, uncles, grandparents and friends got to see the park from the vantage point of a horse-drawn carriage, as Timmy, proud and fearless, shuttled them through the woods.

Over the next few years, as our auto-body repair business continued to grow, Butch had less and less time to spend with Timmy. I barely had time for one horse, never mind two, but a chance encounter with another rider on the trail provided a solution. I happened to mention I was looking for someone to ride Timmy. She told me she had a friend who had a horse as a child and wanted to start riding again now that her own children were grown. I was a little leery, but agreed to get together with the two women the following Saturday. "Well, Timmy," I told the big gelding that night, "hopefully you will have someone to fuss over you again."

Saturday morning arrived, and I walked out to the barn to greet this stranger, hoping I was doing the right thing. The two women were waiting for me. Wait, could it be possible? Could that be Gini, the childhood friend I hadn't seen in 30 years? It was.

"Gini, it's me, Linda!" Gini looked at me, recognition, disbelief and astonishment in her face. "I heard your family moved off Long Island years ago," I told her. Now here she was, living just 15 miles away. We both began to cry. The poor woman who had arranged the meeting was dumbfounded. What a wonderful reunion! And all because of an elderly Tennessee Walking Horse.

Gini and Timmy were riding partners for several years before she bought her own horse. By this time, Timmy was nearly 35. Though he was still healthy and looking good, I didn't want him to pull the carriage anymore or to go out on long trail rides. Once again, luck was with us. Another friend offered to take over Timmy's exercise program. Sophie enjoyed long walks in the park, and now she would take the gelding with her, leading him on foot while her 7-year-old daughter, Sara, sat snug in the saddle. Butch remarked, "With all those women fussing over Timmy, no wonder he's doing so well."

Timmy turned 39 in the spring of 1997. Butch and I had sold our business. We were preparing to move to a 55-acre farm in North Carolina when I got a phone call from an old riding buddy. Knowing I had a Tennessee Walker, he wanted to tell me about a Walking Horse who had been abandoned at a nearby stable. "Doc" was 18 years old but a "nice little horse," and the stable owners didn't want to send him to auction.

Who would want an aged Tennessee Walker? Me, of course. I picked up Doc, a smaller version of Timmy, and brought him home. Of course, my first horse was long gone by this time. I now had Samson, a 7-year-old Clydesdale/Thoroughbred cross. The three horses made the trip to North Carolina with no problem. How wonderful it was to stand on my new porch and watch Timmy and Doc and Samson grazing peacefully in their large pasture.

A year later, the moment arrived that I always knew would come. Timbrooks rolled and couldn't get up. Several hours and the efforts of many neighbors were not enough to raise the 40-year-old gelding. He seemed comfortable, and we fed him apples between attempts to lift him. I never saw pain or fear in his eyes. He was actually looking for the hand with the apple. However, he made no effort to get up on his own. I knew it was time. The veterinarian concurred. When the end came, it was peaceful.

Yesterday, the mail lady brought a heavy box to the front door. I signed for it and saw Gini's return address on the label. I opened the box. There lay a beautiful headstone, engraved in capital letters: "ALWAYS IN OUR HEARTS—TIMBROOKS 1958-1998."

Thank you, Gini. And thank you, Timmy, for bringing my old friend back to me. Thank you for teaching Butch to drive, for sending me Doc. Thank you for pulling our family and friends through the park and for carrrying Sara safely on your back. Thank you for your extraordinary presence in our lives.

VALIENTE'S LAST STAND

*What do you do when the rulebooks you live
by say your best friend must be sold at auction—
probably to the slaughterhouse?*

BY MERRI MELDE

"Greenhorn ranger," the old gray packhorse called Valiente was saying with his eyes, "we can't make it up this steep hill." His sides were already heaving; he'd been walking without pause just below an 8,000-foot pass, and his load of 200 pounds was growing heavier with each step. But no one saw or listened to his wisdom.

Up ahead, Red Top, the saddle horse carrying the fledgling forest ranger named Tim, was sliding back six inches for every step he took in the loose scree. When the lead rope tightened, the ranger didn't even glance back. Old Valiente let out a deep breath closely resembling an exasperated sigh, then he lifted his heavy feet and started upward, resolutely continuing to do his job.

Tim leaned far over Red Top's neck as the horse scrambled to get solid footholds, thrusting his head forward, pushing with his hindquarters, throwing all power forward. Red Top paused, perhaps contemplating some doubts of his own, but Tim urged him onward, upward. This was no trail, but it would be a shortcut for the three of them. It was a challenge. They'd clambered a hundred feet up the slope before something made Tim think to turn and look back at Valiente.

The old horse was down on his knees, panting heavily; his load was too heavy, the ground too loose, the grade too steep. A nauseating bolt of fear froze Tim to his saddle as he realized there was nowhere for Valiente to go but downward to disaster, and there was nothing left to do but watch the events unravel, slowly and sickeningly.

Valiente struggled against gravity and talus and his inevitable fall. He tried to heave himself to his feet; but as his hind end slipped out from underneath him, the load on his back pulled him right over backward. He rolled neatly up his neck, tail over nose, feet in the air, and crashed down onto his belly, his front legs folded underneath him. The momentum bounced him off the ground again and flipped him skyward. Gathering speed in the air, he crashed down again on the load on his back. Over and over he flipped backward, a gray leaden rag doll picking up speed like an untracked freight train hurtling downhill in an explosion of earth and dust.

At last a boulder broke the momentum of the great rolling body, bringing it to a halt. A sudden, ghastly stillness settled as the dust continued rising. "Oh God, oh God, oh God. . ." Tim chanted as he leaped from Red Top and raced, scrambled and fell his way down to the still, dirt-covered body.

That was 15 years ago. Valiente survived that day with no broken bones, no bleeding gashes, no limp—his only injury from the terrible fall was the loss of a quarter-size patch of skin over one hock. After about 20 dazed minutes, old Valiente clambered to his feet, dusted himself off, and followed a shaken Tim (now on foot) carefully back down to the trail. The wooden frames of the packs—still securely lashed to Val's back—were smashed but the contents were intact; even the dozen eggs remained unbroken.

Now Valiente is grayer, and maybe a bit slower, but he still has the same class, the same imperturbable air, and the same intelligent look in his eyes. Not one nick on his strong body belies the wilderness challenges he has met and survived in two decades of faithful service to the Forest Service. Tim and Valiente had become great friends once Tim realized that Valiente was the instructor and Tim his pupil. Together, they spent more than a decade on the trails, encountering bears, calming panicked horses, finding and comforting lost hikers. Val had a good life as a ranger's horse.

But now Valiente faced a different sort of danger, one that was harder for an old horse to understand. He no longer had the strength to carry a full load, but he hated to be left behind when the other packhorses pulled out, so he received easier duties as a riding horse. He carried Tim willingly, but even so, his arthritis made hills a struggle, so Tim often led his friend on foot, to spare him the pain. Finally, even Tim had to admit that Val couldn't work another season; he'd be turned out with the pack string for the winter, then retired.

But the Forest Service can't afford to keep retired packhorses on pasture, where a tired old fellow could relax after decades of hard work. And he couldn't be given away. No, the Forest Service has to follow the rulebooks written by the U.S. government, and the rules say that retiring horses must be sold at auction. And, for a 28-year-old gelding with arthritis, auction would almost certainly mean a one-way trip to the slaughterhouse. The rules would be enforced by people who couldn't possibly understand a horse like Valiente.

Tim and the other rangers pored over their options. Perhaps they could go to the auction and outbid the killer. But how would they haul Valiente home? And where would home be? All the rangers were seasonal workers with no permanent addresses; somebody would have to pay for Val's upkeep.

Maybe Valiente would sense the need to die on his own at

pasture—the easiest, best, most poetic way for a gallant gelding to retire from this earth. Not likely. Val wasn't in the least bit ready to depart. Arthritis couldn't stop him from looking forward to—and expecting—his next season of work. He wasn't about to let his humans down by dying.

Tim wasn't about to let Val down either, not after a lifetime of faithful and generous service. He had to find a way to spare his friend the terror of that final van ride. Still, rules were rules, spring was coming, and the options were growing short.

Then the day came when Valiente stepped into the auction ring. Rockslides, flooded creeks, bears—Val had faced many dangers with fortitude and grace, but a horse who spent his life breathing clean mountain air can be frightened by crowds and air that is full of dust and noise, bad smells and bad feelings. But Val could see Tim standing by the ringside, so everything must be OK.

Beside Tim were two people Valiente had never seen before. They were an older couple, friends of Tim's, who had a home with many acres tucked away somewhere back up in the mountains. Those friends had agreed to follow Tim to the auction in order to buy an old horse, take him home, and let him live out his days with dignity. Everyone had followed the rules.

Valiente is still out there, turned out with another retired packhorse. Whenever Tim comes to visit, Val puts on a show—tossing his tail in the air and getting up to a gallop just to show he still can. No one knows if he occasionally misses his old work, but Valiente has a new job now. How much rest can an old horse get when there are deer to stalk, hawks to count, pastures to mow, and mountains full of fresh air and sunshine to soak up?

FOSTER FATHER

An old gelding finds a new calling when a nurse mare can't be found to care for an orphan foal.

BY REBECCA GIMENEZ, PHD

When a bay colt named Oliver was born one fine spring day in 1999, no one suspected that he was about to break all the rules of commonsense nursing care.

Oliver was born at the Clemson University Equine Center (CUEC) in Clemson, South Carolina, with the assistance of Poag Reid, DVM, the attending veterinarian. It was a difficult birth, but everything seemed fine as Oliver's mother, Bingo, began licking her new little miracle. The youngster soon clambered to his feet and suckled his mother's first milk.

Students at the CUEC observe all newborns and their dams for signs of colic or other abnormalities, so when Bingo suddenly began colicking violently about six hours after foaling, help was at hand immediately. Even so, the mare was dead within an hour and a half. An autopsy showed that, during birth, the foal's hoof must have torn the mare's uterine artery, causing a hemorrhage into the uterus that no one could have noticed because there were no outward signs of trouble until it was too late.

Now the CUEC staff faced another problem: What to do with this very confused and hungry foal? Finding a nurse mare for an orphan foal was the obvious answer. But, at the time, all the other mares on the premises had their own young and healthy foals, so none could be expected to accept this newcomer. Even so, the veterinary staff tried to introduce Oliver to a mare with another foal. She could not be trusted alone with him, however, and neither foal was getting enough milk. So on his third day, the students started bottle-feeding Oliver replacement formula every hour or so around the clock. This kept him well-nourished, but food was only part of the problem. It's not healthy for orphan foals to become too dependent on people because they need to learn how to socialize with a herd of horses—something their mothers normally teach them.

Help with this second problem came from an unlikely source: a 31-year-old Quarter Horse gelding named Tuffy.

After retiring from the Clemson University student riding program, Tuffy had found gainful employment at the CUEC as a baby-sitter for the weanlings. Each year, he taught a new crop of youngsters where and when to eat, drink, groom each other and graze, and he stood over them while they slept. His friendly attitude helped teach the youngsters to look forward to human visitors, with their brushes and attention, and Tuffy patiently tolerated his charges' antics, even when they chewed on his tail and mane.

Tuffy seemed like a good choice to serve as companion to Oliver, but the old gelding had never been close to a 3-day-old foal before, and no one was sure how he'd react. Under the close supervision of Pat Evans, the farm manager, Tuffy and Oliver were introduced. When the tiny foal attempted to suckle every part of Tuffy's body, the patient gelding simply ignored the annoyance. Since the union produced no dire consequences, the two were placed in a foaling stall for constant observation by the students. Within a few hours, Oliver was stretched out in the bedding, asleep, and Tuffy was dutifully standing over him.

Over the next few days, Oliver learned to drink with gusto from a bucket of milk replacer brought out to him by the students, and he and Tuffy were relocated to a large grassy paddock. Tuffy seemed to take his parental duties seriously, nickering to the foal just as his mother would have. The old gelding also patiently followed Oliver as he explored his surroundings. Within two weeks, Tuffy and Oliver were turned out with a gentle mare and foal to see whether they would accept the unlikely pair; they did. Slowly, the number of mares and foals turned out with Tuffy and Oliver was increased; Tuffy demonstrated clear protectiveness for his young charge, steering Oliver away from the other mares. Yet Oliver had the opportunity to interact with other foals and live outside just like any other horse on the farm.

A few months later, I was visiting Reid's clinic when he mentioned a frustrating case. He was working with a mare who had refused to accept her day-old filly, Tike. Again, no nurse mare was available. I suggested that Reid call the CUEC; perhaps Tuffy would accept yet another orphan foal.

Tuffy did indeed willingly extend his parental care to Tike. Oliver, however, was not happy to share Tuffy's attentions with his new little sister. The colt tried to intimidate the filly and push her around. But whenever "big brother" bullied Tike, she ran to the other side of Tuffy, and the old gelding protected her.

Once Oliver was "weaned" and moved to another pasture with other youngsters his age, Tuffy continued to care for Tike in pasture with the mares and foals. Although Oliver and Tike are the first to greet visitors to their pastures, the two motherless foals are about the same size as their peers and are treated like any other member of the herd.

Tuffy's success as a "foster dad" inspired Pat Evans and her assistant manager, Suzanne Elkins, to begin training another gelding, Murphy, to help Tuffy with the baby-sitting and to serve as his successor. Murphy has been living with the yearlings since he was diagnosed with navicular disease at age 4, and he has proved to be an excellent role model. Like Tuffy, he teaches the youngsters manners, but he's also the rock-solid "big brother" they can run to if they get scared. This year, he was entrusted with the weanlings for the first time, and he is doing an admirable and . patient job.

THE YARD-SALE SPECIAL

*A giveaway pony quickly proves to be a
priceless teacher and beloved pet.*

BY SHERRIE LOGSDON

When my family and I moved from New York to Michigan
seven years ago, I knew it would be hard to leave behind our
many relatives and friends. We especially missed our riding bud-
dies, since we had been very involved with horses in New York.
We knew no one here, so my husband, Tom, and I spent our first
few months driving around the area looking for horses and people to meet.

It was on one of these excursions that we happened to stop
at a yard sale. Some cows were grazing in a field by the house, and
among them I noticed an old, dirty pony. He came right to me
when I wandered over to the fence, and even though his shaggy
winter coat was rather unkempt, he had the sweetest face and
kind eyes. I could tell he had been well cared for. He was just
soaking up the attention I was giving him.

I asked if he was being used, and the owner said, "No." Her
children had long since outgrown him, and he had been retired
for years. I told her that if she ever wanted to give him away to a
good home, I'd be glad to take him, and her response was immediate: "If you want him, take him." Tom and I rushed home to get

our truck and trailer, and when we returned, Sparky loaded right up. It was as if he knew children were waiting.

It was love at first sight when my grandson Andrew, then just 2 years old, met Sparky, and I suspect it was a two-way love: the pony seemed to instantly take to the boy, too. Tom estimated that Sparky was about 35 years old at the time, and he thought the pony might live only another year or two. I think he was trying to prepare me in case he died during that first winter. But Sparky did just fine. It took hours of brushing to thoroughly clean that long winter coat, and every bird for miles used his hair for a nest. We had his teeth floated, his hooves trimmed, and all his shots administered. After thoroughly examining the old pony, the veterinarian declared him healthy and fit for riding. Andrew could hardly wait.

Sparky reveled in the attention. And he quickly proved himself to be a wonderful, trustworthy pony with no vices. Well, not bad ones, anyway. We did discover that he can open a gate that's not shut tight, he can untie himself, and he can open any grain container. More than once he tried to follow the children into the house. You also have to be careful about eating in front of him. He loves sandwiches, and you have to be quick and hang onto it tight because he'll try to take it away from you. This pony can smell a treat miles away.

Andrew did so well learning to ride that I would bring them along on trails. At first I ponied Sparky from my horse while Andrew held on, but as he got bigger it wasn't long before he was off the lead line and doing it himself. Even so, Sparky never left the side of my horse, and he was never anything but gentle and trustworthy with the boy. Such sweet ponies are so hard to find I found myself wishing he were just a yearling. In the back of my mind I was always thinking, "How long will I have this great pony?"

Still, Sparky's health never flagged, and the more children he had to play with, the more energetic he got. In fact, he was doing so well, and he loved children so much, I decided to start offering riding lessons for the kids in the neighborhood. That first summer I had seven students, and of course I kept a close eye on Sparky to make sure we weren't tiring him out, but his energy levels only increased. Over the years, thanks to Sparky's inspiration, we have developed a thriving horse program here on our property—and we are no longer short of friends in the local horse community.

For six years, Sparky has kept a busy schedule. In the winters, Sparky helps the local Girl Scouts earn their Horse Lovers and Horsemanship badges, and for the past three summers, I taught the horsemanship program at a local camp. Of all the mounts, Sparky is the children's favorite. In addition to three hours of daily riding on the trails, Sparky helped me teach the children how to groom, lead, saddle, bridle, bathe and love a pony. But he had a special talent for teaching the children how to tie a slipknot. Any knot that wasn't properly tied would be promptly undone. Not that he ever tried to get away. When he unties himself, Sparky just stands around and waits for you, with an air about him that seems to say "You did it wrong!"

He's 41 now, and age is beginning to creep up on Sparky. He requires a special feed for older horses, and we have the dentist out several times a year to keep his teeth balanced. Last winter he had a brief bout with colic; he was down in the snow, and I couldn't get him up. I called Andrew, who came running. He sat in the snow, gently encouraging his beloved pony, and within minutes Sparky was on his feet. A little Banamine, and he was soon back to his old self. Still we wonder, "How long do ponies live?"

We decided it would be best to ease Sparky's schedule, so we don't use him for summer camp anymore, and Andrew has out-grown him. But full retirement didn't sit well with Sparky. He may look old and tired, but he still has plenty of pep, and he paces and cries if he's left behind in the pasture when everyone else pulls out. Fortunately, we now have two more grandchil-dren, Suzie and Cameron, who are eager to learn to ride him and to love him. I know which of the trio will be happiest: Sparky!

He has been such a joy to so many people, not just our three grandchildren but also the dozens of boys and girls who have learned from him in the past seven years. Sparky is living proof that ponies can be useful at any age—they are often safe for beginners, and they can be so patient and wonderful at teaching awkward hands the finer points of horsemanship. As for Sparky, he thrives on the nonstop attention. He must think he's died and gone to Pony Heaven. And when one day that awful time does come, Sparky will be buried right here in his own pasture.

He may once have been a freebie at a yard sale, but to us this old pony is absolutely priceless.

THE UNSINKABLE DAGGER ALMAHURST

Years after being saved from the killers by his devoted owner, a plucky Standardbred gelding faces down death a second time.

BY NICOLE KRAFT

One, two, three.

Dick Rose stood looking out at the horses in the backyard of his Bowdoin, Maine farm, and counted again.

One, two, three. There were, however, supposed to be four.

Rose had left his horses in the pasture, as he regularly does when he runs errands. After an hour and a half at the hardware store, he had returned. The January afternoon was cold and damp, so Rose decided to bring his charges into the barn early. If only he could round them all up.

So Rose, 71, went in search of his missing gelding, a Standardbred named Dagger Almahurst. Down the frozen field, past the bushes on which the horses loved to nibble, toward the creek that a beaver dam had turned into a makeshift pond.

When he was about 50 yards from the creek, Rose stopped short and squinted into the afternoon sun. He thought maybe he was looking at a beaver, resting amid a broken section of the ice-covered water, or maybe even a log.

He was wrong on both counts.

What Rose had found was Dagger Almahurst, submerged up to his head in the near-frozen stream. The gasp released from the old horseman's lips was drowned out by the frantic whinnying from his 13-year-old pacer, who was stuck fast amid the water and ice.

"All that was out was his head and neck," recalls Rose. "The water was some four or five feet deep. I couldn't barely see his rump. It was hard ice he had walked onto, but the current in the middle must have made the ice thinner, weaker. He was stuck but good."

Rose, a wiry veteran of many a Maine winter, knew he had to free his horse—and fast. His first thought was to expand the hole in the ice, perhaps allowing Dagger to pull himself to safety. Despite several minutes of frantic chipping, the gelding was no closer to getting out. Rose knew it was time to call for help.

His next salvation attempt came with neighbor Mike Peterson and some length of rope, as the pair tried to pull the big bay to safety with ropes—to no avail. It had now been nearly half an hour since Rose had found his horse. The temperature continued to drop, and Dagger was beginning to give up.

"We were spending too much time, and the water was ice cold," says Rose. "We couldn't do anything to get him loose, so I finally called the fire department. I got a dispatcher in another town, and he had to call the department right up the street. That took them another 25 minutes to show up. This girl arrives dressed as a fireman. I said to her, 'I hope you're not the whole crew.' Dagger was getting awful weak. He was trying to go under. I had to hold his head up. His eyes were closing, and I could feel he wanted to slip away."

The lone firefighter was soon joined by five others from the Bowdoin Fire Department. After some consultation and consideration, the firefighters used ropes and brute strength to pull the gelding onto the banks.

There he lay, his eyes closed and rolled back in his head, barely breathing, soaked to the skin with ice crystals clinging to his body. "I thought he was dead," Rose recalls. But he was not willing to give up on his old friend. He dropped to his knees and immediately began to massage the horse's body and legs. Dagger's back legs were so stiff with cold they could barely bend, so Rose worked methodically at them to warm the joints and enable them to move. All the while he implored, "Do it for your grandfather this one time, get up on your feet!"

It took three minutes for the pacer's eyes to open, prompting Rose to take him by the halter. Then, he says, "It was like the Lord said 'get up!'" Dagger scrambled to his feet—albeit with a bit of a lurch—and looked around at his surroundings, as if surprised to find himself on land. "We put the blankets right to him and walked him right to the barn," says Rose. "It was like he'd had too much to drink, he was wobbling so."

Hugh Townsend, PhD, a professor in the Department of Large Animal Clinical Sciences at the University of Saskatchewan's Western College of Veterinary Medicine, says Dagger was well-equipped to handle his frigid circumstances. Townsend, who is working on a study investigating increased incidents of hypothermia among donkeys, says that condition in horses is quite uncommon because of their physical makeup. "By and large, horses deal with the cold extremely well," he says. "They are insulated by their coat to a degree, as well as their fat cover. Also, the digestive process in the horse, as in the cow, is a large fermentation vat—involving both the cecum and the large intestine. That produces a lot of heat. That helps to keep the core temperature up."

Townsend added that despite the appearance of ice on

Dagger Almahurst's legs, they were not "frozen" in the true sense of the word, for he was surrounded by water that was still in liquid form. "What happens with frostbite is that the blood in the vessels clots (thromboses), but you have to go below freezing," he says. "If water will flow, it is not at freezing temperature, and that means that blood is not going to freeze. Salty water actually freezes at a lower temperature than fresh water, and salty water is pretty much what blood is. I'm sure the horse was very cold and stiff, and it wouldn't surprise me that the horse would look a bit funny when walked."

The gelding's struggles into and out of the ice had left him with "wicked cuts" on his hocks, knees and under his legs, to which Rose applied disinfectant and Furacin salve. He started Dagger on a course of sulfa, which later gave way to more powerful antibiotics, as well as a course of Banamine. "He couldn't hardly walk on the hock. It took a week or so for it to come down; his knees looked like footballs," says Rose. "Under his chest was all swelled—he looked just like Dolly Parton!"

But, says Rose, "He never stopped eating—his appetite was good the whole time. He was awful lame, but he was quick to recover."

Recovery seems to be Dagger's middle name, as this is not the first struggle he has had to overcome. A son of Pacing Triple Crown winner Ralph Hanover, Dagger Almahurst has been plugging away at the racing wars since 1990, when as a 2-year-old he made six unsuccessful starts. He raced every year thereafter—sometimes making nearly 40 starts in a year—competing in Canada, Florida and Maine.

Rose, who works full-time as an elementary school custodian when he is not caring for his horses, four cats and various stray and wild animals, met the pacer in February of 1997. Dagger was on his way to "the killers," and Rose was approached with the opportunity to buy him.

"They wanted $600 and said they couldn't [earn] a check with him," says Rose. "I looked at him. He was a cute little thing. He'd had a bowed tendon, but he looked OK. I figured, what's $600? It was love at first sight if you believe in those things."

Dagger showed his appreciation for his new home by starting to earn money almost immediately for his new owner. In their first year together, Dagger brought home about $6,000. In 1998, he earned more than $8,000 and followed up with $6,560 in 1999. In his 11-year career, the bay has won 28 of 309 races for lifetime earnings of $125,083, and Rose says he fully expects to add to that total in 2001. "He seems like he's coming back good from this; I don't see any reason why he won't race again," says Rose. "He's a tough old guy. I guess we both are."

Dagger is actually one of the more youthful members of the Rose stable, as the horseman proudly cares for his horses as if they were his grandchildren, and provides a longterm and loving home for them. He also refuses to race on anything but "hay, oats, water and maybe some Lasix. His strategy allows his performers to keep competing year after year. "I bought them when they were all middle aged, and I kept them, 'cause they all race good," he says simply. "A lot of people think a horse is nothing but a piece of machinery. When it wears out, you get another. I don't like wearing them out. If I use them right and treat them right, they don't wear out."

Rose says one thing he has curtailed for all his horses is their access to the backyard and the dammed creek. He says the horses have ample room in the other pastures so there is no reason to tempt fate another time. And he doesn't want to interfere with the beavers' natural habitat.

"People want me to trap the beavers, but I don't bother with them," says Rose. "I love all these animals. The beavers are just doing what beavers do. Those horses never went into that creek before. I don't know what got into him."

As for Dagger, he has enjoyed his newfound celebrity. He was featured in the *Portland Press Herald* and even received a $10 check days after the incident from a woman who wanted to buy him a bag of carrots.

"I never thought I would ever see the day that horse would be in the barn again," says Rose. "I'm not the most religious person, but I did some praying that day. The Lord must have helped us. Dagger is a lucky boy. He's a great little fella."

A Priceless Gift

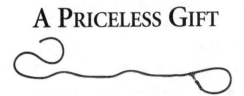

An aged and ailing pony named Clyde rewards his tireless keeper with lessons that will last a lifetime.

By Marla Kay Svoboda

The sights, sounds and scents of our hometown's annual rodeo filled the air, and everything from the scent of sweaty horses to the bellowing of the bulls to the song "Should Have Been a Cowboy" piping over the loudspeakers was filling everyone with "cowboy" spirit. Over the cheering crowd, I heard my friend Laura calling me, asking "Hey, are you still looking for a gentle pony for the kids?"

With my three small, wide-eyed children gathered around, I said, "Yes!" And that was when we first heard about Clyde.

Laura's fiancé, Lee, is an equine dentist. One day when he was working in a huge horse barn, Lee came to the last stall. Looking in, he asked the owner what work the Shetland needed. The owner said not to bother; the animal was too old to invest time and money on. The pony had spent his prime years pulling carts for handicapped children, but now those productive days were behind the old pony and he'd been banished to the back of the barn.

Nonchalantly the Shetland's owner said, "You can have him if you have any use for him." Without hesitation, Lee brought the dispirited pony home, where Laura patiently nursed him until he had the strength to whinny again. Because he looked so much like a miniature Clydesdale, Laura dubbed the pony "Clyde."

Visions of a spirited, energetic pony filled all of our heads the first time we drove out to see Clyde. My kids wanted a horse of their own that they could handle without the constant supervision required when they rode my "big" horses. When we pulled into the driveway to meet this fine animal, there stood Clyde, shining from a recent bath, tethered to a trailer having his hooves gently trimmed.

"Ohhh-nooo!" was my first, disappointed thought when I saw him. "Look for the positive," I whispered to myself. But the more I inspected the pony, the more warning signs I saw, and the more discouraged I became. Clyde had cataracts on both eyes; one was severe. He also had a swayback, hollowed eye sockets, persistent sinus drainage and many missing teeth.

"Isn't he beautiful!" Laura declared proudly. "He's 20-plus years old, but Shetlands have great stamina, and the kids should be able to ride him for quite a few more years." I wondered if we were looking at the same pony. I did concede that Clyde's hearing was good; his ears were pricking, and he was tilting his head to catch the sounds of the unfamiliar children scrambling around him. Laura offered to sell him for $150—just enough to cover their expenses since they found him.

I pulled my husband and children aside for a private conversation. Clearly, this wasn't the sassy pony any of us had envisioned, and even the kids weren't sure they wanted to take Clyde home. By all appearances, Clyde's life was approaching its end, and I wasn't sure I wanted to put my kids through the heartbreak of losing him. My husband, always the diplomat, pointed out that Laura was obviously proud of this pony, and she'd done a lot of work to get him back into even this condition. "We don't want to hurt her feelings, so just buy him," he said. "It's another chore, but how much longer can he last?" And so, reluctantly, we loaded

Clyde for the journey to his new home.

That was three years ago. We never did let the kids ride him. We tried each one on his back for several minutes on that first day he came home, but his old joints were popping, and he was struggling to keep his balance. That was the last load he was asked to carry. It was time for Clyde to retire.

We now suspect that Clyde is in his late 30s, not his 20s as we originally thought. He is completely without sight in one eye now. He still occasionally experiences sinus drainage, and his joints seem to pop more with each passing season. Lee still comes out to trim his hooves and check his teeth, but with every checkup his teeth show more deterioration. The grass is increasingly difficult for Clyde to chew. Grain that once gave him energy boosts and fat seems almost impossible to chew and digest properly. Nebraska winters are hard, and it is time-consuming to carry him warm water and expensive to buy him the special grain and nutrition blocks he requires now. By most definitions, Clyde is useless, caring for him a chore.

But he and I have gotten to be great friends. His care was a challenge at first, but as the love and trust developed between this old pony and me, the challenge turned into a privilege. Clyde has subtle ways of rewarding me. He gives me a sense of accomplishment when he gains a little weight, and I can pat myself on the back for whipping up a new and improved feeding program for him. He also gives me a sense of gratification, knowing I am helping him to live the last years of his life with comfort, compassion, companionship and love.

Clyde is no longer in the pasture with my other horses. Last summer he was given freedom to roam our farm. This allowed him to eat the nutritious sweet clover and alfalfa growing near the house and seek out the most tender grass wherever it might be growing on the farm. I am happy and relieved to say that Clyde seems to be maintaining his weight, which he'll need to get him through another long, cold Nebraska winter.

He sleeps near our patio window at night, where he can watch his devoted family inside. Each morning, I find him standing on the front steps with my dogs and cats, waiting to shadow my footsteps as I do my daily chores around the farm.

I think Laura feels bad for having sold us a "lemon," as she put it. But, as she told me on that day when we bought him, "I know he'll never have a better home or more care than what you will offer him." I sincerely thank Laura for her kind heart and for offering Clyde to us. I respect Lee for being concerned enough to have brought this old pony home in the first place. I'm grateful to my family for their support and understanding of the expense and effort it takes to maintain Clyde. But most of all, I salute Clyde for constantly reminding me of what determination and a steadfast will can endure.

Clyde is content now, and he is welcome to live out his remaining time with me. Despite his years of neglect, I can see that he has a sense of belonging on our farm and of being cared for and loved without condition. I know he won't live too much longer, and his death, when it comes, won't be unexpected or devastating, but he will be tearfully missed. For now, though, I take time to enjoy my old friend each day.

I never knew Clyde in his prime. But on these calm autumn days, when the leaves are turning the colors of fire and an aromatic breeze sweeps across the alfalfa, Clyde picks up his little head and swings his tail. Just for a few moments, I can see the years melt away, and I catch a glimpse of my Clyde as a colt again, stout and strong, only beginning his life. His youth may be long behind him, but his determined soul, unending will and golden heart are sound and intact; these are the qualities that will be impressed on my memories forever.

THE GENTLE GIANT

In a brief time, a huge horse with a secret past left a lasting impression on the family who loved him.

BY DEBRA HAMMONS

I first saw him in a stockyard where we'd been told there was a horse available who was cheap and gentle enough for my young daughter. My immediate reaction was a mixture of awe and disappointment: At well over 17 hands, he was one of the tallest horses I'd ever seen, but he was also one of the most pathetic: It seemed as if every bone in his body showed clearly under his unkempt coat, and his feet were overgrown, dry, chipped and cracked.

Just as we were turning away, I noticed how interested he was in my nephew. We hadn't been able to coax the horse over to us, but he had gone to Clayton and was allowing the small hand to stroke his great nose and face. I warned the boy to be cautious, but at the same time I was amazed at how careful the horse was with him.

I found myself taking a closer look. None of the cracks in his feet seemed to be very deep, and he didn't limp. His legs were all straight and clean. His mane and tail looked full, thick and healthy. And what a wonderful face! His ears were small and well shaped, and his bright eyes were set perfectly on his massive head. Clearly, this was a fine, well-bred animal who had seen better days.

The yard owner knew nothing about the horse but guessed his age to be 16 to 18 years old. My husband, Coy, and I discussed whether we really wanted to take a risk on an unknown horse in such bad condition, but even as we tried to talk ourselves out of it, I think we both had already decided—Sampson would be coming home with us.

It didn't take long for us to realize how special Sam was. Despite the dark and the strangeness of the new place, he unloaded like a dream the first night. We gave him food and water, and he settled right in; no exploring or nervous "new home" jitters, just eating.

Over the next months, he accepted without hesitation everything we did or asked him to do. Endless grooming, fly spraying, farrier work, veterinary visits—he stood and watched everything we did with a quiet, almost amused, look on his face. Despite his great size and strength, we could move any part of his body with the touch of our fingertips. He acted like he had seen and done everything and really wasn't impressed. Coy once said that if Sam could speak, his only word would be "So?"

Once Sam began regaining his condition, we started to ride and exercise him. I've owned several horses in my life, and with each one, there was always something to teach. I never found anything that Sam didn't already know. He responded instantly to every cue I used, as if it was second nature. Sam clearly once had been very important to someone; his impeccable training must have required immense time and patience as well as kindness and skill. I don't think he'd ever been scared or hurt, and the more I learned about him, the more I wondered how anyone could ever have let him reach such a state of neglect.

Sam improved daily. With steady riding and good food, he

became quite handsome. His dull winter coat gave way to a silky, brownish-red one, and although his feet were never perfect, they too improved.

We spent many wonderful days together that summer, riding every inch of the mountain trails and roads around our house. Sometimes I would bridle Sam, throw a blanket over his back, and let my daughter, Brandi, ride for hours around our pastures. I kept a watchful eye on her when she rode alone, but Sam never violated my trust, despite Brandi's lack of experience. Once, as I watched them walk across the field, Brandi became totally lost in some dream and seemed to completely forget she was riding. As her thoughts wandered further and further away, Sam's pace became slower and slower, until finally he stopped. He stood for a few seconds, then turned his neck around as far as he could to watch her, waiting until she remembered where she was and what she was doing, before he would move on.

But my brightest memory of Sam was the fall morning, more than a year later, when I took a day off from work. After sending kids to school and Coy to work, I was faced with two choices: clean the house or go for a ride. I chose the ride.

Sam and I had a slow and relaxing stroll toward a town three miles away where my parents own a small country store and cafe. My father and some locals were gathered on the front porch when I arrived. They all commented on how good Sam looked, and one said that the first time he'd seen Sam, he'd though we'd been crazy to buy such a skinny, ugly nag. Then he said, "You wouldn't want to sell him, would you?" I laughed and told him that never again would Sam be for sale.

We continued our ride down to the post office before turning back. Passing the store again, I saw my father alone on the porch waving to us with one of Sam's favorite treats: my mother's homemade biscuits. My father was raised on a working ranch, and he has tremendous respect for horses and a store of knowledge you don't get from books. I value his opinions, and what he said to me that day elated me: "You've done good by this horse. He's a nice animal and, heck, I never thought he looked half bad."

All the way home, I enjoyed Sam's strong, even pace and admired the beautiful coat and the giant shoulders moving smoothly and gracefully. I thanked him for being a horse I could trust so completely and for being such a good teacher for my daughter. I told him of my plans and dreams for him, of new skills he could teach Brandi, of trail rides and camping trips, and of how Coy and I were taking farriery classes so we could take better care of his feet. I made him promises: that I would always love and care for him, that he would always have a home with us, and never again would he be hungry.

Once home I gave Sam an extra-special grooming. I bathed and dried him, combed every tangle from his mane and tail, and brushed him until his whole body seemed to glow. Sam and I had had many rides together, but none had ever left me so happy. I'm glad I didn't know then that I would never ride the big horse again.

The pasture grass was nearly gone, so the next weekend we moved the horses to another field where they had been many times before. Everything was fine when we checked them on Saturday. We were away for the day on Sunday and didn't return till long after dark, so Coy said he'd check them again Monday morning.

"Sam's hurt." The tone in Coy's voice told me it was bad when he called me at work that morning. "You need to come home and we'll decide what to do. I don't think the veterinarian can do much."

It was an hour and a half before I could make it home, and just as I pulled in, Coy was leading Sam up the driveway. My heart sank. Sam was having a lot of trouble using his hind leg, which had a deep, jagged gash running down the back from his hock to his pastern. He and Coy were both exhausted from the short walk up from the pasture.

The veterinarian was out on another emergency call, but his office assured me he would come as soon as possible. We cleaned Sam's wound as well as we could. Caked with dirt, rocks, grass and bugs, the wound was swollen and looked infected, but most alarming was the proud flesh. I couldn't believe so much could grow in such a short time. It was at least two inches thick and six to seven inches wide—maybe more. It boiled up from the middle of the wound and exploded around his leg, and it looked like a mound of rotting hamburger. My hands shook as I tried to comfort Sam, who obviously was in a lot of pain.

When the veterinarian arrived, he gave Sam some shots, and we shared the horse's relief as his pain finally was subdued. It took hours for the veterinarian to cut away the proud flesh and clean the wound. He left Sam with a huge pressure bandage that ran the length of his leg and instructed us on how to care for the wound. We followed his instructions faithfully for a week, but when he returned for a follow-up visit, he told us he wanted to take Sam back to his clinic where he could treat our horse more aggressively.

Two weeks later I called to check on Sam for the hundredth time. The veterinarian's voice seemed very small and distant when he came on the line. "Mrs. Hammons. We need to talk." A heavy, dark feeling settled deep in my heart, and I dreaded the drive to the clinic. When I got there I sat in the parking lot for a few minutes summoning courage to go in. He was waiting for me in the lobby, and he led me into his office and closed the door.

Sam had not responded to any treatment, and the leg continued to deteriorate. The mass had become a cancer-like tumor, devouring more and more of Sam's leg, which was now useless. The veterinarian didn't think further treatment would be of any value, but he was willing to keep trying if we wanted.

It took awhile for me to answer him—not because I didn't know what I would say, but because I knew how much the words would hurt: "No more. Sam's been too good of a friend to let him suffer any more."

The veterinarian wouldn't have the help he'd need to do the job until tomorrow afternoon, so I promised we'd be back first thing in the morning. The drive home was a blur. The only thing I remember for sure is that's when the guilt set in. I had never stopped believing Sam would recover, and I was determined to do everything I could to help him. But now I had to face the possibility that by not checking on him until Monday we had not only prolonged his suffering, we had also cost him his life. I felt I had broken all my promises, and the pain consumed me.

The next morning, Coy and I stopped to get a basketful of Mom's biscuits, still warm from the oven, and we drove to the clinic in silence. Sam greeted us when we entered the barn, and as I approached, I tried not to look at the leg, which was a horrific sight. Slowly I fed him all of the biscuits, and when every crumb was gone, we gazed at each other for a long moment. I laid a hand on his great forehead, and closing his eyes he lowered his head and pressed his face gently to my chest. Over and over I told him how sorry I was, and how much he would always mean to me.

I didn't remember Coy leaving the barn, but when I heard his voice outside, I knew the veterinarian had arrived. A hundred panicked ideas jumped into my head. Could Sam live with three legs? Could we make him a fake one? Surely there was another veterinarian who knew how to help him. Maybe we should wait another week. Or two. Or three.

All of the maybes and doubts dissolved when my eyes fell

on the terrible leg. There was no changing this reality. I stroked him again as I said my last goodbyes.

It's been almost two years now, and little things like finding a piece of forgotten tack can still bring a tear to my eye. But more often I remember Sam with a smile.

Many of our friends and neighbors still wonder why we took a chance on such a big, ugly, skinny horse, and few ever saw his true worth. But I have a secret I'd discovered only a few days after Sam came home: He was tattooed! The numbers under his upper lip were, to me, proof that I'd not been crazy and that someone else had also once valued Sam as much as I did. At first I wanted to track down those numbers and find out where Sam's life had begun, but over time, that became less important. His training told of good owners, but somewhere along the line he had slipped into a life of neglect. I just didn't want to find out that Sam had been sold because he didn't run as fast or jump as high as someone had hoped he would. Whatever were the great plans and dreams Sam carried at his birth, to me and my family, he was always a winner.

Horses will always be part of our lives, and I now have a big, black Tennessee Walker I think the world of. But he holds a different place in my heart, far from Sam's, because Sam's spot is reserved for that one special horse who comes along only once in a lifetime.

DIAMOND IN THE ROUGH

Devoted care and sensitive training turn a vicious
filly into a top-notch cow horse.

By LYNN ALLEN

I was wasting time at a livestock auction when I spotted a crowd around a pen. I wandered over to see what the attraction was: A dark gray filly stood in the center, her ears flat back, her head aggressively "shooing" away anyone who leaned too close. Every time someone climbed up on the fence, her lips skinned back and she pounded with her front feet. Her eyes weren't rimmed in white, they were red.

"Broke at, and screwed up," said an older horseman I respected. He had also stopped to see the side show.

"Think she'd come around?" I asked.

"Depends on how bad she's been messed up and how much time you're willing to put in." He stared through the fence at the hostile filly. "She'll go for slaughter. Anything you have to do to make her come around would save her life. If she's too bad, you could always sell her next horse sale."

I'd seen enough of her teeth to know she was about 3 years old; her front incisors were just growing in. Her hooves showed signs of long-term care, but not recent trimming. Someone had pulled her mane and clipped her muzzle within the last 60 days because the hair had grown out about an inch. Nobody trims the feet or clips the muzzle of a snapping, kicking outlaw. This terrible attitude had to be a recent problem. There was a halter impression on her nose, but no saddle or harness marks on her skin.

I occasionally try to rehabilitate spoiled or abused horses and take on colts with problems. Most of the time I succeed; sometimes I don't. There are horses who are fit only for dog food, and I've found a couple. With her big eyes, dainty head and signs of long-term care, this filly looked like she might be worth a try.

I bought her by the pound after she chased the ring man over the fence and threatened the auctioneer on the block.

My latest rescue mission didn't seem to appreciate her new home. She spent the next two days trying to chase me away from the gate with her teeth and front feet. I could see it would take only one mistake to be badly hurt by this horse.

A little research into her past revealed the name of a local trainer renowned for single-day, roundpen break jobs. His high-pressure methods had backfired on this filly; she fought back. When he jumped the fence to escape, attack became her motto.

After giving her a couple days to settle in, I started trying to reshape that motto. Her pen was hot and I gave her extra hay so she would be thirsty. Later, I carried her a bucket of water. When she lunged at the gate, I left with the water bucket. Every hour or so I offered her water, and each time she threw her head at me, ears back, teeth snapping. And each time, I turned around and walked away.

"It's for your own good, sweetheart," I told her. "You're glue if you don't learn to get along with me. I'm your last chance."

By late afternoon she was thirsty. As I approached the gate, she eyed me angrily, but didn't flip her ears back. I stepped in and she threw her head up, stomping her front feet. I took the bucket back out. Immediately, she dropped her head and looked at me, ears forward. She wanted a drink, and she was starting to figure this game out. I stepped back into the pen. Her eyes tightened, but she didn't threaten me.

Moving slowly, I set the bucket down and stepped back, keeping the fiberglass stick I carried for protection hidden behind my back. Carefully, she reached for the bucket, ears forward, watching me out of the tops of her eyes. She grabbed a gulp and jumped back. I stood there quietly, hands at my sides, never looking directly at her and trying to keep my body relaxed. She slipped up and grabbed another gulp. She threw her head up. I ignored her and she drank the small bucket dry. The second bucket didn't require any theatrics. For the first time I saw a glimmer of hope for my little dragon.

Two days later, I informed her that if she wanted to eat, she would have to take fresh grass out of my hand. Her flat ears told me she wasn't taking anything from me. Eventually, her tummy outweighed her pride and that was another blow to her independent nature. Her stare was more baleful than angry now.

At the end of the week a client called, wanting to send me a horse to work. My little dragon wasn't ready to quietly accept a halter, but I needed the round pen. Curiosity brought another friend to help catch her; he'd been hearing stories. Finally, after an hour of dodge-the-horse's-feet, we gave up trying to sweettalk her and dropped a rope over her head. She had been roped before; she immediately turned to face us, ears flat. We gently reeled her in and put a halter on her. No surprise, she was broke to lead, but resentful about being forced. We left her in the round pen wearing a halter, a leadrope and a red-eyed glare. I was discouraged by her reaction, but my friend seemed to think I was making progress.

The next morning, I explained that she was going to pick her own grass, but only if she let me lead her to it. She didn't try to evade me when I approached her, but then escape had never been her strategy. I scratched and petted her a bit, ignoring her red eyes, but watching her teeth and feet. When I was sure she wasn't going to try to use me for new bedding, I led her out to a nearby field. She pulled a bit and bounced, but she didn't lunge or strike. At first she was too nervous to graze and shifted around me restlessly, watching me suspiciously, but finally she settled down enough to snatch a few bites of the knee-deep alfalfa. When I took her back, I turned her onto a bigger pen with such amenities as a shade tree and a water trough. Now that she was out of the hated roundpen, most of the aggression disappeared, but the contemptuous attitude remained. Three times a day, I caught her and took her out to graze and after four days, she was still insolent. We were making progress; she wasn't attacking me anymore, but her independent streak needed some more work before she could be useful.

The next morning, when I walked by her pen she gave me her challenging glare. I left. At noon, I walked by again and she glared at me. I caught the colt in the pen next to her and took him out to graze. She hung her head over the fence and watched us. By evening her glare softened into a quizzical stare as I led the colt past her to the field. When I put the other horse back, she walked along the fence next to us and nickered.

She stood quietly while I walked up to her and picked up the rope. Her head was up, but her ears weren't flat, and her muzzle wasn't pinched. I let her graze, and this time she didn't try to stay at the end of the leadrope. She even let me scratch her withers while she ate. When I put her away, I gave her a flake of alfalfa hay and left her munching, her eyes soft and quiet. The next morning she was waiting for me at the gate, ears forward, a welcoming nicker moving her muzzle.

Now I was happy with her progress; two weeks from violent

to willing. Such an attitude change deserved a reward. I named her Dusty. I only name horses I intend to keep.

Since roundpen training was not an option with Dusty, we started an alfalfa-field training routine that included lots of space and free time. This horse firmly believed in the fight-instead-of-flight theory, and introducing something new without upsetting her was a challenge. Most horses will take about anything if there's grain around, but not this one.

It took a week of grooming before I could walk up to her and touch her with a brush without getting a glare.

It wasn't until her grazing spot was out of grass and I took her across the road to a bigger patch that I found her weakness. She was interested in everything and wanted to get out to see the world. Now I was her partner in discovery and the only security she had, and she began to actively look forward to our training sessions. I took her away from the barn before putting a driving rig on her. She was too busy looking around to worry about the strange thing on her back. Ground driving was easy, she stepped right out to see what the world contained as long as I was with her.

Finally, when she was quietly accepting everything I asked or offered, I climbed on her back. For a moment I thought I'd made a serious mistake; Dusty's eyes turned red, her ears flattened and she shifted uneasily. I talked and scratched and petted and finally, she bent around to smell my foot. When she stepped off, she was tense, but willing to give this new thing a try. A week later, she was ready to be introduced to her new job as a cow horse at a livestock auction.

An auction yard can be a daunting place for an inexperienced horse. The alleys are narrow, and the cattle have to squeeze past the horses to get to the pens. I rode another horse and ponied Dusty so she could see how things were supposed to work, but the noise, confusion and pressure worried her; there was red in her eyes. She willingly followed the first bunch of cows to their pen, but when we turned around and met another bunch face-to-face, she couldn't see any way to avoid them. The dragon awoke and she stood in the middle of the alley, throwing her head and stamping her feet, threatening the cattle. I talked quietly to her as I pushed her over against the fence and protected her with the body of the bigger horse.

Once she understood that the cows would go by if she stood near the fence, I tightened her cinch and swung on. Dusty was chasing cows under saddle, a little worried, but quite willing to bite a slow old cow if necessary.

The next auction day, the horseman that had hauled Dusty home for me a month earlier stopped by to talk. Leaning on the fence, he glanced over at my gray filly as we lined up with the other horses to wait our next batch of cattle.

"That's a nice little gray. Who ya riding her for?" he asked, reaching over and petting her neck.

"You ought to know her, you hauled her home for me," I told him.

He frowned at me, "Awhhh." His disbelief was strong in that one syllable.

"How are you doing with that nasty thing you bought?" he asked, changing the subject.

"No, really. This is her," I insisted. "She wasn't as bad as she looked."

"Awhhh." The skepticism was even stronger, but he looked her over a little closer as we turned after our bunch of cows and trotted down the alley.

He watched her over the next hour while we penned cattle and he talked to the riders. Dusty and I were closing the gate coming out of a side alley when the loudspeaker blared.

"Bullpen. One bull to a bullpen."

Still green and slow work with gates, Dusty was still in the alley when the barn gate opened and a big red bull lumbered out. He wasn't shaking his head or being threatening, so I told Dusty to stand next to the gate and wait for him to go by. Irritated, the bull didn't go completely around us. He plowed his shoulder into Dusty's rump.

I felt him connect and Dusty staggered into the gate. I tensed, sure she was going to panic and bolt down the alley, probably bucking. She didn't bolt. She threw her head up, her ears swept back and her eyes turned red. Before the bull could push past us, she jumped forward and launched both hind feet at him. She kicked him twice more before he lumbered out of range. Ears still flat, and not the least bit excited, Dusty stomped over to her place in line, eyes still red and her lip curled.

"Well, there she is! There's that nasty little bronc," sang out my friend from his side of the fence.

A year later, Dusty still believes in fight instead of flight and she doesn't back off from a nasty old cow or bull that threatens her. If the red eyes and teeth don't send them on their way, she swaps ends and kicks.

Dusty is one of my success stories, and if I had walked away from those red eyes and snapping teeth that day, I would have missed out on one of the best cow horses I've ever ridden. She was truly a diamond in the rough.

Illustrations by Pamela Wildermuth